Personal conversations

International Library of Psychology

Editorial adviser,
Clinical psychology:

Kevin Howells
University of Birmingham

Personal Conversations
Roles and Skills for Counsellors

Gerrit Lang

and

Henk van der Molen

with

Peter Trower

and

Roger Look

Routledge
London and New York

First published 1990 by Routledge
11 New Fetter Lane, London EC4P 4EE

Simultaneously published in the USA and Canada
by Routledge
a division of Routledge, Chapman and Hall, Inc.
29 West 35th Street, New York, NY 10001

Typeset directly from the publisher's word-processor disks by
NWL Editorial Services, Langport, Somerset, England

Printed in Great Britain by
Richard Clay Ltd, Bungay, Suffolk

British Library Cataloguing in Publication Data

Lang, Gerrit, *1934 –*
  Personal conversations : roles and skills for
  counsellors.–(International library of psychology)
  1. Counselling psychology
  I. Title II. Molen, Henk van der, *1954–* III. Trower, Peter,
  1938– IV. Look, Roger V. Series VI. Psychologische
  gespreksvoering. *English* 158'.3

Library of Congress Cataloging in Publication Data

Lang, G. (Gerrit).
[Psychologische gespreksvoering. English]
Personal conversations : roles and skills for counsellors / Gerrit
Lang, Henk van der Molen in cooperation with Peter Trower,
Roger Look.
p.   cm. – (International library of psychology)
Translation of: Psychologische gespreksvoering.
Bibliography: p.
Includes indexes.
1. Counseling. 2. Helping behavior. I. Molen, Henk van der,
1927– . II. Title. III. Series.
BF637.C6L3413   1990   89–10379
158 '.3–dc20   CIP

ISBN 0-415-03477-9
ISBN 0-415-03478-7 (pbk)

'. . . neither the whole of truth nor the whole of good is revealed to any single observer, although each observer gains a partial superiority of insight from the peculiar position in which he stands.'

William James 1899

Contents

Preface   xi

1 Introduction   1
  Purpose and structure   1
  Who can the counsellor help with this approach?   3

Part one: Insights into helping

2 The helper's philosophy   7
  Introduction   7
  Typical attitudes of friends and relatives   8
  The philosophy of the helper   12
    The diagnosis–prescription model   12
    The cooperation model   16
  The sophisticated helper   20

3 The client-centred approach   23
  Introduction   23
  Rogers' theory   25
    Self-actualization   25
    Acceptance   25
    The origin of problems   26
  Rogers' method   27
    Unconditional positive regard   27
    Genuineness   27
    Empathy   28
  A critique of Rogers' theory   31
    Is Rogers too optimistic?   31

Contents

Is Rogers' theory too vague? 32
Is Rogers' theory really essential? 33
A cognitive theory of experiencing 34
Experiencing as an active process 34
The role of feelings 37
Does Rogers really regard experiencing as passive? 40

4 The social learning approach 41
Introduction 41
The social learning perspective 42
How is behaviour learnt? 43
Learning through modelling 43
Learning through the consequences of actions 45
How is behaviour regulated? 47
The influence of expectations 47
Influencing expectations 48
Self-regulation 48
Processes of self-regulation 49
The tyranny of the ideal-image 50

5 The helper at work 54
Introduction 54
Clarity of goals 54
The roles of the helper 57
The confidant 57
The communicative detective 60
The teacher 65
The coach 66
A helping model 69
Problem clarification 69
Gaining new insights 70
Treatment of the problem 72
The model in practice 74
Cumulative building of goals and tasks 74
Applying the stages to problems 75
The model is not all-powerful 75
Time is limited 76
The helper as a person 78
A good human being? 78
A suspicious person? 81
Self-protection 83

Part two: Skills and strategies for helping

6 Problem clarification   89
  Introduction   89
    Goals of the initial interview   91
    Basic attitude and basic skills   91
  Starting the interview and making an initial contract   93
  'Non'-selective listening skills, attending behaviour   95
    Non-verbal behaviour   97
    Verbal following   100
    Silences   101
    A retrospective view   102
  Selective listening skills   106
    Asking questions   106
    Paraphrasing of content   110
    Reflection of feeling   112
    Concreteness   116
    Summarizing   120
  Regulating skills   122
    Goal-setting and goal-evaluation   123
    Situation clarification   124
    Thinking aloud   129
    Ending the counselling interview   131

7 Gaining new insights   134
  Introduction   134
  Making insightful connections   135
    Interpretation   135
    Interpretation as a skill   137
    Giving information   141
  Differentiating skills   142
    Advanced accurate empathy   142
    Confrontation   145
    Positive relabelling   149
    Examples of one's own   153
    Directness   154

8 Strategies for treatment   158
  Introduction   158
  Treatment   158

The client's own attempts 158
Levels of treatment 159
Goal-directed action 163
Formulating goals 163
Steps in an action programme 165
An example from practice: treatment as education 167
Treatment as education 171
Termination 172
Referral 172
The client does not want to go on 174
The helper does not want to go on 175
The goal has been reached 177

Appendix Videotapes 179

References 181

Author index 185

Subject index 187

Preface

In writing this book we have two major aims. The first is to investigate the processes involved in counselling a person with a problem. A wide range of factors must be considered and a number of important questions addressed if we are to appreciate the fundamental nature of the helping relationship. Thus, for example, what are our goals in helping someone? How do our views on the way in which people function influence how we deal with them? How does the relationship between helper and client affect what is achieved? *Insight* into these crucial aspects is needed if we are to improve our own helping skills. Part I of this book deals with the theory behind the helping procedure and gives the reader a framework from which to work.

However, to *know* what is necessary for good helping is not enough. We should also be able to *do* and *say* the right things in the right way in practice. Hence Part II of this book describes in detail the *concrete skills* needed to help someone with a personal problem. Learning these skills is a necessary condition for effective counselling.

The principles expounded in this book have emerged from a decade of practice and research into effective counselling conducted in Holland and England. During this time workshops in counselling skills have been developed for both professional helpers and for those whose work entails a degree of helping or advising others, including teachers, dentists, nurses, policemen, negotiators in industrial disputes, careers advisors, pastoral workers, and management trainees. For all these and other groups the principles and skills presented in this book have been found to be relevant and effective and we therefore feel that workers in all occupations with an interpersonal component will find that the skills presented will help them to become more effective communicators. Furthermore, we believe that the principles outlined are applicable in any situation where one person is helping another, so that anyone who has ever considered the question, 'How can I help a fellow human being in distress' will find much of use in this book. With this in mind the book contains little esoteric material and we have tried merely to unravel and systematize the things people do more or less implicitly when they attempt to help others with their problems.

The book explains in everyday language, with as little jargon as possible, the interpersonal skills necessary for the effective discussion and solution of problems. Unfortunately, one often finds in professional training programmes that these interpersonal skills, which are so 'ordinary', are neglected in favour of more impressive technical skills. While not wishing to denounce the importance of the latter we believe that help with personal problems is not an area reserved solely for professionals. Having greater education and experience does not automatically mean that one does a better job of helping.

Throughout this book the counsellor is referred to sometimes as she and sometimes as he. The choice is based purely on the need for clarity and to avoid the cumbersome use of she/he or he/she etc.

This book is the result of intensive cooperation between authors from two different countries: Holland and England. It is a revision of our Dutch book entitled *Psychologische Gespreksvoering* (Lang and Van der Molen, 1984), which has proved to be useful to many kinds of helper in the Netherlands and Belgium.

We would like to thank Mrs P. de Waard-Dekking for the first translation of the Dutch text. This translation was the basis for the present book. Finally, we would like to thank Kitty Lenstra, Ali Pestman-Schrage, and Ingrid Slothouber-Mannoury for their cooperation in the preparation of the final manuscript.

Gerrit Lang,
Henk van der Molen,
Peter Trower, and
Roger Look,
October 1989

Chapter one

Introduction

Purpose and structure

At various times in our lives, most of us find ourselves helping another person with some personal problem. This is an important and, in many cases, a very difficult undertaking. There are no simple answers to the question of how best to help another person overcome difficulties. In some cases help may just not be possible, and at other times even when we believe that we know what is good for the other person we find that he does not heed our 'sensible' advice. It is, therefore, easy to become pessimistic about the possibilities of helping people and to adopt a fatalistic view that endeavours to help are bound to fail. However, this book is based on the fundamental assumption that in many cases effective help is possible and that in most instances a helper does not need a long and rigorous professional training to be able to provide such help.

The first aim of this book (Part I) is to investigate the processes involved in counselling a person with a problem. The second aim (Part II) is to give a detailed description of the concrete skills needed to help such a person. Concordant with our stated aims in Part I (Chapters 2–5) we examine the theory underlying our form of counselling, while in Part II (Chapters 6–8) we go on to describe the nature of effective helping skills, which are based on the theory chosen in Part I, and discuss how these are put into practice.

In Chapter 2 we present a basic philosophy for working with people on their personal problems. The frame of reference in which we approach the client and his problem is of obvious importance in influencing how we actually work with them in practice.

Having discussed our basic premises we go on, in the next two chapters, to consider theoretical viewpoints which we believe are important in guiding what we actually do and say during the helping process. In Chapter 3 we pay attention to approaches based on 'client-centred' theory (Rogers 1951, 1957). We expand on this Rogerian viewpoint to include principles drawn from the field of cognitive psychology and we particularly advocate the work of Wexler (1974) as an important complement to basic counselling theory. Theories of social learning (for example Bandura 1977; Mischel 1968, 1973) have been widely used in explanations of the development of personal problems and we shall investigate how such theories may be incorporated within overall counselling theory in Chapter 4.

Thus the book has a somewhat eclectic character as regards the choice of theories. In recent years theorists (for example Wachtel 1977; Garfield 1982) have begun to make attempts to integrate the various different helping approaches by searching for factors common to all such approaches. In doing this some integrationists (such as Garfield 1982) have sought commonalities in processes of helping (for example the building of the helping relationship), while others (for example Carkhuff 1969a, 1969b) have investigated similarities in the characteristics of the helpers themselves in an attempt to discover which qualities and skills are essential for good helping. We hope to show that the theories we draw on are complementary and that their integration increases the flexibility and effectiveness of counselling.

As well as the aforementioned theoretical backing a helper should have in mind an overall structure to guide him in the counselling process. The counsellor should normally have a goal in mind and in order to achieve goals in a systematic way he needs a step-by-step approach which allows him to monitor his progress. The helper should also be able to modify his approach towards the client at various stages of the process in order to mirror the changing nature of the counselling relationship and tasks. To this end in Chapter 5 we present four 'roles' of the helper and describe a model of counselling based on the work of Egan (1975, 1982). In this model we distinguish various stages of counselling, describe the goals of each stage and the skills needed to achieve each goal. We then focus on the helper as a person and discuss the core qualities of the effective helper.

In Part II we describe the microskills of helping and the integration of these skills into an effective style at each stage of the counselling process. This is in line with the philosophy of this book: it is not enough to know what we want to achieve in counselling, we must also have the skills to bring this about in practice. Though the theory of counselling is not inherently difficult it is this application of theory to practice which is often a stumbling-block.

Chapter 6 describes the nature and function of a number of basic skills needed to conduct a counselling interview. In this the counsellor is principally a listener and guide and aims to clarify and bring order into the client's account.

Chapter 7 deals with more complex skills which build on those in Chapter 6 to promote clearer or even new insights into the client's problems and help to prepare the client in the search for solutions.

In Chapter 8 we discuss the process of working out solutions to problems and then implementing these in the real life situation. Since there are many kinds of problems, all of which demand their own treatment and specialist knowledge, we will restrict ourselves to a number of general principles and directives for the helper. The final question discussed in this chapter is how to end the counselling relationship.

Who can the counsellor help with this approach?

What type of client do we have in mind for the form of counselling advocated in this book? Without resorting to labels we believe that this kind of counselling is of most use in helping people whose psychological state is such that they can still be held responsible for their actions and are capable of looking at their problems in a more or less objective fashion. While the problems such people have may seem relatively minor to an outsider, to the person himself they may seem totally insoluble and of major importance. The sense of calm and security that counselling offers helps the person to begin to put his difficulties into perspective and to work out solutions to them. Thus we are addressing our counselling efforts to people who can cope with their problems themselves but not *by* themselves.

In the initial stages of counselling psychological accessibility may be quite limited as the agitation and confusion caused by the problem is very great. However, in the course of talking to someone who remains calm and relaxed in the face of such distress the client's agitation should abate fairly quickly and he should begin to be able to discuss his problems lucidly. Where the person's anguish is such that the counselling approach is not effective in reducing his discomfort to bearable levels the emphasis should lie on forms of crisis-intervention to which we can only refer here (for example Bellak and Small 1978).

As its title implies this book is about *dialogues*. In particular it is concerned with situations where one person turns to another (who may or may not be a professional helper) because he wants to talk about things which are distressing him. We therefore start with an assumption that the person in distress has at least a minimal willingness to discuss his problems. This does not necessarily mean that such a discussion will progress smoothly as a willingness to talk and the ability and courage to do so are quite different things. However, the person indicates by his initiative that he trusts the helper sufficiently at least to make an attempt to talk about his difficulties. How profound such a dialogue actually becomes will depend on the way in which trust develops during the ongoing counselling relationship.

While in this book we restrict ourselves to discussing counselling for individuals, it is our belief that elements of our basic programme are equally relevant to counselling with married couples, families, and groups. However, counselling in these sitations may require more specialist skills than we provide in this book.

Finally, we would like to underline that although our emphasis in this book is on the counselling process and the need to encourage the client to tackle his problems himself, this does not mean that we consider the solution to all problems to lie exclusively within the individual. Often it may be necessary to change the client's environment or the system within which he lives. Nevertheless we believe that even when this is the case the liberating effect of gaining insight into one's problems and learning skills to cope with them will enable the client to be more effective in seeking changes in his social situation.

Part one

Insights into helping

Chapter two

The helper's philosophy

Introduction

When a counsellor engages in the process of helping someone with his personal problems she is faced with a whole series of questions. What does she think ought to be achieved in the counselling enterprise? In what direction should solutions be sought? The answers to these questions depend largely on the specific problem, but we should also be aware that the personal philosophies of both the helper and the client will strongly colour such answers.

In order to be able to answer these questions, the helper must take a certain stand. This cannot be objectively determined but is a personal choice which is influenced to a considerable degree by the helper's own ideas and beliefs as to how people should behave towards each other. We therefore believe that an investigation of the helper's philosophy is a necessary starting-point in understanding the process of counselling. We can illustrate some important points with the help of dialogue from a fictional case. In doing this we can compare the reactions of friends and relatives with those of professional helpers in order to get a better idea of similarities and differences. We are going to choose the case of Michael, a university student, who is struggling with a problem and seeks help from a number of quarters. Let us hear how Michael describes what is troubling him.

> I've been at college for a couple of months now but I don't feel that I'm doing very well. It was all right at first but I soon found that I was having difficulties concentrating on my work. I manage to get down to studying sometimes but I find my attention wandering and I worry that I have chosen the wrong

course. Perhaps I'm getting worked up over nothing – after all, it's still early days. I wonder how other people cope? Ah well, I'll stick with it, I'm sure most people must have problems to start with. On the other hand if I'm not going to like it perhaps it would be better to start looking for something else straight away. Oh! I'm in a real mess.

We can see that Michael is worrying about his studies. He needs to talk about it, but how?

Typical attitudes of friends and relatives

With some hesitation and uncertainty Michael starts a conversation with a friend:

I've been worried about my studies just lately – I don't think I'm doing very well. I just can't seem to concentrate and I've already failed a couple of essays. Perhaps I should find out whether I could change to another subject. What do you think?

It is evident that Michael's words lack conviction, both the tone and content displaying his uncertainty. People often begin like this when they feel hesitant and are unsure whether they should bother somebody with their problems. Michael's friend reacts:

You shouldn't worry so much, I'm sure you're doing fine. The first year is always pretty boring and lots of people fail essays. I've been finding it difficult to get down to work myself but, after all, we have only just started. Anyway, don't let it get you down – there's a good film on tonight, do you fancy going to see it? We could go down the pub afterwards.

Of course, this is only one way in which the friend might have reacted and the reader will be able to think of various alternatives. Nevertheless, this type of reaction is common and in this case several aspects of it might prove helpful to Michael: reassurance, encouragement, well-meant advice, and an offer to go out socializing together. Perhaps an evening on the town will help Michael to start the next day afresh, at least mentally.

What does the friend's reaction teach us about people's implicit beliefs about the best way to help others? First, it is evident that the friend takes a firm hold of the situation: 'You shouldn't worry so much, I'm sure you're doing fine.' Thus he takes a very clear and direct approach. He listens to Michael's problem and without much further deliberation offers his solution. He almost tries to force Michael out of his worries: 'There's a good film on tonight, do you fancy going to see it?'

Analysing the interaction between Michael and his friend a bit more deeply it is possible to distinguish the motivations of both parties. Michael wants to talk about his problem but does not want to be considered a worrier by his new friend. Hence the casual, rather vague way in which he puts over his concerns. He is uncertain how his friend will respond and thus he tentatively tries to 'sound him out'. His task in doing this is made more complicated by his own uncertainty as to the true nature of his problem.

Michael's friend, for his part, feels the need to distance himself from Michael's problem. He has also been aware of the possibility of failure but has attempted to push such thoughts to the back of his mind. Although he publicly claims to be able to cope, his private conviction may not be so great. Perhaps he has no real solutions but feels under pressure to produce some anyway, as this is what Michael seemingly wants. Thus the friend may give the impression of treating the matter much more light-heartedly than he actually does.

The dialogue may now develop in various ways. Michael may be heartened to hear that his friend has had similar problems and press him to discuss how he coped in greater detail. He may also agree to the proposal of going down the pub for a few drinks. However, suppose that neither of these courses of action brings Michael any relief. Still struggling to find a solution to his problem he decides to talk to his parents about it. During a weekend at home, after dinner he begins: 'Well, I, uh, . . . There's been something worrying me recently . . . I feel that I haven't been doing very well in my studies and I've been thinking about changing courses.'

Mother: But Michael, you were doing so well, weren't you?
Father: What do you mean 'change courses', you've only just started – I've never heard such rubbish!
Michael: But I just can't concentrate. I've been getting bad marks and perhaps it would be better to change to something else before it's too late.

Michael wants to say more but he feels that what he has already said has gone down badly with his parents who have not seemed very sympathetic. He thus becomes even more vague and uncertain of himself. His father, who is just about to leave, says:

Well, you should think it over very carefully but I don't see the point of giving up so soon. The trouble was that everything was too easy for you at school. Now you have to work a bit harder you don't like it and want to give up straight away. No, you should keep at it for at least a year and then see. Everybody has setbacks, you know, you will have to learn to cope with disappointments like everybody else.

While this is only a brief summary of the conversation, the gist of it is clear. His parents have gained some understanding of how Michael feels. However, their reactions are influenced by a number of other factors. From the father's responses we get a clear impression of his fundamental beliefs: 'You should not change your mind once you've made a decision.' 'Once you have started something you should keep at it.' 'You should be able to cope with disappointment', etc. He thus tries to appeal to Michael's sense of responsibility. 'You should think it over very carefully.' In a firm manner he suggests that Michael should stop thinking in a negative way and should continue his studies at least until the end of the year.

How should we evaluate the type of help that Michael's father gives? If you believe that Michael should be encouraged to discuss his problem further within an atmosphere of trust and support then you would probably feel that his father takes the wrong approach. He gives Michael little opportunity to express his doubts and uncertainties and he does not seem to be interested in his son's worries. Why not? If we try to view the situation from the father's perspective we might consider that the father has a strong personal investment in having a son who is a good student and works hard to achieve success. Furthermore, he sees that it is in his son's best interests to have the same aspirations. Thus bearing in mind that the father's words are spoken with some emotion, we can see that he at least displays a sense of involvement and a feeling of joint responsibility. An indifferent 'Well Michael, you do what you think best' would not be very constructive. In short he demonstrates that he cares for Michael's welfare but uses a method that is ineffective for helping Michael to solve his difficulties. It is notable that he gives rather ambiguous messages, so, for example, 'You should think it over very carefully' implies that he has a certain amount of freedom to act according to his own convictions, while 'No, you should keep at it for at least a year' suggests that such freedom is restricted. The dilemma of how directive we should be in counselling deserves further consideration. In our culture we place great value on the individual's right to make his own decisions and to shape his future as he chooses. Thus it is held that decisions should be taken on the basis of one's own motives, particularly where personal problems are concerned. Nobody can decide for somebody else what is the best way for him to live his life. While we endorse these views they do create a dilemma, for what should one do when one sees a friend or relative acting in an apparently unwise, stupid, or irresponsible manner? In such cases one may be less likely to espouse the high-minded ideals described above. The existential literature has discussed in some detail this problem of feeling the need to take responsibility for a person while still leaving him a freedom of choice. De Beauvoir (1948) says about it:

> by a tacit agreement, by the very fact that I am solicited, the strictness of my decision is accepted or even desired; the more seriously I accept my responsibilities, the more justified it is. That is why love authorizes severities which are not granted to indifference.

> (de Beauvoir 1948: 137)

So de Beauvoir believes that a concern born out of love allows a person to take a more directive line in helping. However, this should not be taken to the extreme of justifying authoritarian behaviour in the name of love. We often do not know beforehand which decision is the right one for the individual but even when we do the question remains whether or not we should interfere: 'To want to prohibit a man from errors is to forbid him to fulfill his own existence, it is to deprive him of life' (de Beauvoir 1948: 138). This quotation infers that in general we should be very careful not to protect a person too much with the result of a lessening of his own sense of responsibility. If having taken responsibility for his actions he fails in a certain endeavour, then this is viewed as a painful but essential and integral aspect of human experience.

The dilemma of how much responsibility to take for another person's welfare is nowhere better exemplified than in the parent – child relationship. Most parents want to promote a sense of independence in their children but also fear that too much independence will lead to the child 'going off the rails'. This fear, born of love, frequently turns parents into authoritarian tyrants who allow their children very little true freedom.

We have emphasized these difficult points for several reasons. In the first place we wish to show that, especially for people close to him, the right course of action to take in helping an individual is often very unclear. Second, we feel it important to point out that authoritarian behaviour is not always inspired by lust for power or domination but often by a sense of responsibility and care for another person. Furthermore, deep friendship or love may lead to such overconcern that they become a barrier to effective helping. Similar difficulties may exist for the one with the problems. He may be inhibited in talking freely to loved ones because of a concern not to worry or inconvenience them.

The reader should not conclude from the above that the discussion of personal problems with a friend or relative should be avoided. We have merely pointed out some of the obstacles in the way of effective helping by discussion of the reactions of close friends and relatives in a particular case. In the next section we shall discuss the nature of the professional helping relationship and how this differs from the more informal type of helping we have discussed so far.

The philosophy of the helper

It may be somewhat simplistic to speak of 'the' philosophy of the helper, as naturally there are as many philosophies as there are helpers. However, in order to enable the reader to look more closely at his or her own belief system and to compare this with those of others we will discuss two broad 'types' of counselling. In doing this we will use the following questions as guidelines. First, what is the helper's own basic philosophy and how does this affect how she works with the client? Second, how does she stimulate the client to search for solutions to his problems? Third, what are the helper's own motivations in the helping process?

The diagnosis–prescription model

Let us assume that after talking to his friend and his parents Michael still feels no closer to sorting out his problems. He has discovered that his friend also has some difficulties studying and that his parents do not favour him switching to another field of study. However, these reactions have not encouraged Michael to talk further about his problems. Nevertheless, his nagging uncertainties about whether he is ready for the demands of the course lead him to seek the help of the university careers service. He calls and makes an appointment. On arriving at the careers centre he is handed an extensive questionnaire with items on his education, hobbies, family background, and reason for consulting the service. After completing the questionnaire he is shown into the main waiting room. He sits down and waits: what will happen? He hopes they will be able to help him here as he no longer feels able to cope with the situation himself. He consoles himself that he will be talking to an expert who will surely be able to tell him what to do.

A kindly-looking woman enters and invites him into her office. She sits behind her desk and asks Michael to have a seat opposite her. After introducing herself she gives a brief explanation of how the session will proceed: first they will talk about his problems for forty-five minutes, followed by some short tests and finishing with a further discussion. A report will then be sent to him. Then she says:

> To start with I would like to find out more about why you are seeking advice at the moment. Can you tell me more about how you are feeling?

Michael: Well, yes, you see I'm not doing very well at my studies and I've been thinking that perhaps I've chosen the wrong course. I don't know whether I should carry on or change. That's what I really need advice on.

He stops and looks hopefully and a little helplessly at her.

She: I see . . .

She looks thoughtful. Michael waits in silence, seeing that the counsellor is struggling with his problem.

She: Tell me, how many hours a day do you study?
Michael: Well, apart from lectures, about two hours if I'm lucky.
She: And sometimes you don't get much done because you can't concentrate?

Michael: That's right.
She: I see. [Thoughtfully] So you are wondering whether this lack of
concentration is due to you having chosen the wrong subject?
Michael: Yes.

The conversation then proceeds along familiar lines with the careers
counsellor asking the questions and Michael answering (mostly with
brief responses). When the forty-five minutes are up, Michael is
shown into another room to take a series of short paper-and-pencil
tests and finally has another brief talk with the counsellor. She asks
him some more questions and tells him that she will send her report
by mail. Michael is satisfied and goes home much more optimistic
than when he arrived.

What is the careers counsellor trying to achieve with Michael?
This is not at all clear in the light of what we have already discussed.
Although she begins by inviting Michael to talk about his problems
she quite quickly takes over the initiative herself. Her overall approach, moreover, leaves little room for Michael to express his own
thoughts and feelings. By dealing with him in this way the counsellor
is implicitly implying that there is a general standard of sensible behaviour which Michael should follow and on which she will base her
interactions with him.

How does this counsellor go about stimulating clients to seek appropriate solutions to their problems? If, as seems the case, she believes that she knows what is 'best' for the client, she probably does
not feel a need to talk with the client for long to get an impression of
his wishes and opinions. To her, what is 'best' for the client is choosing a profession in which the client is likely to achieve success and
which fits his apparent interests. To help her in making a well-
founded judgement she has at her disposal psychological tests which
enable her to collect relevant data.

So what happens in the interview is that Michael is rapidly being
changed from a person talking with a careers counsellor into an 'object of research'. This may sound rather harsh but Michael does not
seem to resent this process and indeed hardly notices it: isn't this
what he came for after all? He wanted to hear from the expert what
is 'best' for him and this is what he was given.

How does the careers counsellor come to take up the mantle of an
'omniscient expert' examining an 'ignorant' client? We can see the
process taking place very quickly in the interview. The counsellor

says, 'I would like to find out more about why you are seeking advice.' Michael tells a little about himself and then states that he just needs advice as to what he should do next. He looks rather helplessly at the counsellor and it is obvious that he is expecting support and concrete suggestions. The counsellor for her part may have expected more from Michael but she senses his distress, feels appealed to, and is visibly thinking about the next step. At this point Michael stops talking altogether, he can see that the 'expert' is thinking and believes it would be impolite to interrupt her! On further questioning Michael's replies become shorter and shorter. Thus in less than a minute the roles have become very clearly delineated. The careers counsellor develops her own views on the sources of Michael's difficulties. These views are based on her experiences with similar cases which she has seen. For this particular case her frame of reference is refined and sharpened by a series of questions. While the counsellor thinks and actively tries to find a solution to his problems Michael just does what he feels is required: answer questions. Finally, having diagnosed what is causing Michael's difficulties, the counsellor presents a recipe for their solution.

Although this careers counsellor may personally believe in complete independence and freedom for individuals in making their own decisions and would strongly defend their right to make choices based on their own standards, in her professional work she chooses a role which apparently leaves her clients little room for taking part in the process of self-determination.

The major danger involved in this 'diagnosis–prescription model' is that the need of the helper to appear to be an expert in her field may lead to a too goal-directed and simple approach to what might be very complex problems. We can see that by controlling the conversation herself and leaving the client little room to express his own ideas, the 'expert' avoids the risk of being sidetracked or of being faced with problems which she does not feel sure how to handle. She thus reduces the chances of losing face and losing control of the situation. The fear of a more open and involved way of working with clients often leads either to a distancing from personal material or to a too premature definition of problems and their solutions. Clients frequently complain that the helper made up her mind about the problem before really finding out what was wrong.

Empirical studies have also cast doubt on the effectiveness of the diagnosis–prescription model of counselling. Lewin (1958) has investigated the effect that information on nutrition given in a directive way had on the eating habits of housewives. He discovered that in most cases the information was just ignored. Later studies have confirmed these results (Korsch and Negrete 1972). However, the same studies have shown that where the approach to the individuals concerned has allowed for more openness and greater communication, the advice given was much more likely to be followed.

We have produced a number of arguments to suggest that the diagnosis–prescription approach is not very helpful when dealing with personal problems. We will now turn our attention to another approach which we believe enables us to work so that the client's autonomy is respected and we do not impose our own set of norms on to him.

The cooperation model

Let us return to our previous example and pick up the thread with Michael awaiting the arrival of the careers counsellor. However, this time we will present a different approach.

The counsellor takes Michael into her office and offers him a chair.

She: Well, Michael, you called us to say that you wanted to talk about your problems studying. I would first like to tell you a little about the way that we work here. In this first interview, which will last for about three quarters of an hour, we shall look together at your difficulties and find out what are the main issues. After that we shall discuss the best way to continue. Does that sound O.K. to you? [Michael nods] All right then, could you tell me why you have come to see me?

Michael: Well, yes, you see I'm not doing very well at my studies and I've been thinking that I've chosen the wrong course. I don't know whether I should carry on or change. That's what I really need advice on.

He stops and looks hopefully and a little helplessly at her.

She: So you're feeling a bit uncertain about what you should do. Could you tell me a little more about what all this means to you?

This is a difficult question for Michael to answer as he still feels quite confused about his problems. While he considers his answer the counsellor looks at him kindly, attentively, and expectantly. Michael starts to talk more about his studies and mentions the discussions he has had with his parents and friend. Seeing that the counsellor is paying attention to what he is saying he gradually finds it easier to describe his doubts, worries, convictions, and plans. At intervals the counsellor gives him feedback on the themes he has outlined and he begins to gain a better idea of the key issues which are bothering him. Michael is also encouraged by the accepting attentiveness of the counsellor which makes him feel that his problem is not ridiculous or trivial and that something can be done about it.

This, then, is a brief sketch of the beginning of the conversation. There are marked differences from the previous example in which the counsellor took a diagnosis–prescription approach and we shall discuss these differences using the framework we have previously employed.

What is the counsellor's philosophy of the way people should lead their lives? The *content* of someone's activities and behaviour (that is, what they actually say and do) is not a matter which she will talk about in a prescriptive manner. However, she does have beliefs about the *way* in which people should shape their lives, and these beliefs are linked to the existentialist view we have described earlier. In particular, she believes that people should be encouraged to be self-reliant in searching for solutions to their problems. While it may be objected that this is a standard similar to those imposed in the diagnosis–prescription model it is more about form (that is, how to choose what to do) rather than about content (what to choose to do).

If, then, the counsellor wants to promote self-reliance, how does she go about achieving this? Part of her task must be to help people gain a feeling of responsibility for their problems and arrive at possible solutions. In the example we have described something essential happens at the point when Michael, after saying, 'That's what I really need advice on,' stops and looks hopefully and a little helplessly at the counsellor. While the latter shows understanding ('So you're feeling a bit uncertain . . .') she does not take over the problem but says, 'Could you tell me a little more about . . .' The result is that Michael starts to think about his problem in more detail. This is in contrast to the process in the diagnosis–prescription model whereby the helper works out the solution while Michael just waits. However, it should not be thought that the counsellor in the cooperation model is inactive or uninvolved. On the contrary, she actively and attentively helps Michael to think through his problems and in doing this she must be totally involved in the helping process.

A crucial aspect of the cooperation model is that the counsellor consciously aims at achieving an increasing insight into the client's thoughts, beliefs, and feelings. In short, she tries to place herself in the client's experiential world. By doing this she is able to help the client clarify and refine his own ideas and feelings about the matters troubling him. For, if we reject the notion that the helper should prescribe her own standards on to the client, and instead believe that she should help him to produce his own solutions within his own system of norms, it is surely necessary that she should be able to relate strongly to his ways of construing the world. The counsellor does not make the client an 'object of research' but rather a partner in the counselling enterprise. Counsellor and client work together on the clarification and solution of problems: hence the 'cooperation' model.

The effective helper has another goal which becomes more explicit as counselling progresses. By being involved at all stages of the process the client comes to learn about the process of problem-solving so that when he has problems in the future he will be better able to deal with them himself and will not need the advice of experts. Again, this is consistent with the existentialist perspective that each person must freely choose his own way of living. By gaining more insight into the forces influencing us and being better equipped to deal with them we become more truly free in the control that we have over our own lives.

While we have stated our belief that the cooperation model encourages the client to choose freely and responsibly, a number of objections may be raised against this position. Thus, for example, can we truly speak of freedom when the client, who expects advice on how to run his life, is apparently refused that advice by a counsellor who only wants him to find a solution for himself. The psychologist in our example is faced with just such a dilemma. She wants to appeal to Michael's sense of independence and responsibility and does not want to dictate what he should do. However, a major part of his problem is that he is not very independent and finds it difficult to work out solutions to his difficulties. Indeed, what he wants in going to the psychologist is for her to tell him what to do about his study problem. By refusing to accept the client's own choice to leave the decision about his future to an expert, the psychologist is acting against her principles of unconditional acceptance of the client's right to choose. In other words she appears to want to force the client to act in the way she thinks best so that he arrives at a point where he learns to choose freely and responsibly!

The solution to this dilemma lies in an open discussion of this problem between helper and client. In this the counsellor should make it clear why she wants the client to make his own choices and to share in problem-solving endeavours. Only when the client understands this explanation and accepts the underlying philosophy will the cooperation model be likely to succeed. The helper lets the client know right from the beginning how she wants to work, makes agreements with him, and asks for his approval of this way of working. In the example we have described the psychologist indicates early on how she wants to work ('we shall look together at your difficulties') and asks Michael for his approval ('Does that sound OK to you?'). Many clients like this approach and will have expected nothing else. Some (like Michael) will not have expected it but agree all the same. In either case the client consents to the cooperation model of working and the helper chooses a role of stimulating the client to work jointly on the problem.

Some clients may persistently resist the cooperation model we have outlined. Despite explanations of the advantages of such a way of working these clients maintain that all they need is advice in order to solve their own problems. In some cases it may be possible for the counsellor to give concrete advice based on her specialist knowledge. Thus a counsellor who has an understanding of the law may be able to give appropriate advice to a client in legal difficulties. When dealing with personal questions, however, such as problems in interpersonal relations, the situation for the helper is quite different. In these cases it is generally inappropriate to proffer advice and the client should be encouraged to participate in the problem-solving process. Where it becomes increasingly evident that the client is unable to accept that the helper cannot solve his problems for him, the latter will have to consider seriously how far she can meet the client's wishes. In some cases the helper may have to take the difficult decision of explaining to the client that she feels that little more can be achieved by their meeting and that their contact should gradually be decreased.

A number of further points need to be made about the helper's role in the cooperation model. Just as in the diagnosis–prescription model, the helper's position towards the client is less personally involved than that of friends and relatives. She is able to assess possibilities and judge likely consequences from a greater distance. This gives the client room to express his thoughts and feelings more freely.

The client doesn't have to be afraid of the consequences. For the counsellor herself this distance prevents her becoming overwhelmed by the client's distress. However, the counsellor's attempts to place herself in the experiential world of the client within the cooperation model are likely to make for a much stronger identification with the .client than within the diagnosis–prescription model. The consequences of this will be discussed in Chapter 5.

The sophisticated helper

It seems as if we have quietly pushed aside the diagnosis – prescription approach in favour of one in which the helper treats the client more as a human being, involving him as a partner in the counselling enterprise and helping him to solve his own problems. However, it may be asked whether such a helper really does treat her clients in a truly human non-prescriptive way. Is cooperation just a pretence? It might be proposed that counsellors who talk about 'cooperation' in the counselling process are really just sophisticated experts who, knowing about the ways in which they can successfully manipulate people, choose the form of friendly cooperation. They advocate a cosy chat and pretend to be 'just friends talking together'. But what goes on in the minds of such helpers? Are they really all ears for the client's story or is more going on? Well, we have already noted that the helper has a number of important tasks other than attentive listening.

Thus the helper tries to bring some order to the thoughts and feelings expressed by the client and helps to put them into perspective. She tries to gain insight into his way of thinking and feeling which together form his frame of reference. By assessing and monitoring the relationship with the client the helper is able to plan the course of the interview so that the client feels at ease while working on his problems. On the basis of a good relationship she will, when she feels it necessary, say things which may be painful or difficult for the client to accept. All in all, then, it is obvious that the helper is active on a number of fronts even if on the face of it she seems to be rather 'quiet'. We should be careful not to equate client-centredness with passivity.

The sceptic may state that at least in the diagnosis – prescription model the helper is much clearer and less secretive about showing her expertise. She presents herself as a detached expert and plays that part openly. In the cooperation model the helper uses her psychological knowledge to create a stimulating atmosphere in which the client can express himself fully. Again, the sceptic might state that there is no real spontaneity on the part of the helper and that she is merely a manipulator who just gives the impression to the client that they are working on an equal footing. Some critics of the cooperation model have even suggested that the model obstructs the development of any real human feeling in the counselling encounter. We believe that these criticisms are unfounded. By describing the approach as manipulative, critics imply that the counsellor is working in a self-interested manner. We hope to have made clear that, far from acting to their own advantage, counsellors should, as much as possible, put their specialist knowledge at the service of the client in helping to overcome his problems. Furthermore, a charge of manipulation implies that the counsellor acts in a stealthly or secretive manner. We believe that this is also unjustified: while the counsellor has a number of aims in the counselling process which are not explicitly stated, these aims are in no sense secret and can be explained to the client at any point. Thus, for example, the counsellor can explain that summaries of important points enable the client to bring some order into the perception of his problems.

When the helper plays her role with wholehearted conviction and directs herself towards the client's goals, she is working in a truly genuine manner. It is the counsellor's job to act in such a way as to best help the client. This demands flexibility and a varied arsenal of skills.

Overall we may conceptualize the counsellor as being at the service of the client, using her individual skills and knowledge to provide as good a service as possible. This is not to say that we believe that there is no such thing as ungenuine helping. Such helping may arise when the counsellor's own self-interests obstruct a truly genuine helping style. Thus it may occur when a helper tries to hide her failures or is more interested in creating an impression that she is an expert than in looking for solutions to the client's problems. We will return to the issue of 'genuineness' in Chapters 3 and 5.

Chapter three

The client-centred approach

Introduction

While upholding the philosophy described in the previous chapter, a helper is still not yet sufficiently equipped to work with clients. He still lacks a system to bring order to what he hears from the client and possibly to interpret it in a way different to that maintained by the client. He also needs a method to motivate the client to search for the solutions to his own problems. The helper requires theories which can place the client's behaviour in a certain context and suggest how he needs to adapt his counselling style to deal most efficiently with the client. Without such a system of theories the helper may find himself lost in the complicated mass of information given by a confused client.

Of course the question which naturally arises is what theories can be considered most suitable to our approach? There is a wide range of theories of personality (for a review see Hall and Lindzey 1978; Hergenhahn 1984) and it is very difficult to judge which one is the best in general. The results of empirical research into the effects of various forms of treatment have not provided evidence for any one clearly superior theory although there are indications that a certain combination of theoretical perspectives and methods may produce an increased effectiveness in the treatment of specific problems (Smith and Glass 1977; Shapiro and Shapiro 1982). In particular the combination of cognitive and social learning theories of problem causation and treatment seems to be especially effective.

The theories which the helper will use to guide him in the counselling enterprise will to a large extent be chosen on the basis of how well they fit into his personal philosophy and his philosophy of helping. We have described our philosophy in Chapter 2 and following this we can propose a number of requirements which an appropriate theory should meet:

1 The theory should emphasize the potential of the client in playing an active part in seeking solutions to his own problems.
2 The theory and the techniques arising from it should be easily explainable to a client.
3 The theory should be broad enough in vision and approach to be applicable to a wide range of problems.
4 The theory should be versatile enough to deal with problems ranging in severity.

On the basis of the above we have not wanted to confine ourselves to one theory. However, we have based our way of working predominantly on the theory and method of the 'client-centred' approach developed by Carl Rogers (1951, 1959, 1961). This theory has many points of contact with the philosophy of helping outlined in Chapter 2. In our opinion Rogers' approach is very strongly influenced by existentialist philosophy. To be quite honest it should be stated that the authors (and probably most counsellors) are not completely certain themselves about the origin of their own philosophy: via existentialism, Rogers' work, a certain spirit of the times, or the working of personality factors? Probably it results from a complicated integration of all the influences.

We will first discuss the main themes of Rogers' theory, explaining their relevance to our own counselling methods. We will then consider the theory outlined by Wexler (1974), a cognitive psychologist of the 'client-centred school', who clarifies and modifies Rogers' theory on a number of points. While Wexler's modification of the client-centred approach provides us with a blueprint of how to conduct counselling sessions, it says relatively little about why people function as they do and how problems actually arise. To gain further insight into such aspects of human functioning we will present in Chapter 4 approaches based on social learning theory, particularly drawing on the work of Bandura (1977, 1986) and Mischel (1968, 1973).

Rogers' theory

Rogers' theory has been described and discussed in many publications both by himself and others. In the following sections we will limit ourselves to the most important concepts inherent in his work.

Self-actualization

Rogers (1951, 1961) repeatedly emphasizes a 'self-actualizing tendency' which he describes as the fundamental motivational force driving a person to develop his potentialities. This tendency to self-actualization should be viewed as directing the person to grow towards an optimal personal ideal. However, this ideal is not static, it is a process of continual development and refinement of possibilities. The course of this development is largely determined by the 'quality' of experiences that the person has. Rogers believes that the quality of a person's experiences increases as that person is better able to incorporate all types of stimuli, both internal and external, without inhibitions or resistance. He states that this optimal form of experiencing will occur naturally, provided that circumstances are favourable.

Acceptance

What does Rogers mean by 'favourable circumstances'? He clarifies this point by introducing the concept of 'unconditional positive regard'. He states that it is of prime importance for a person's development that from an early age he should experience this unconditional positive regard from people in his environment who are important to him. This entails that he should be accepted unconditionally just as he is in an atmosphere of warmth and love. It does not mean that the people around him should be enthusiastic about everything the growing child or adult does but that he experiences an underlying sense of security that he is accepted by them without conditions. This 'unconditional' is the essence of the concept, not: 'If you tidy up your room, you'll be a good girl' but: 'You are a good girl, that goes without saying, but what about cleaning up this mess!' It is difficult to capture the true nature of this type of acceptance in words and examples. It is typified by an atmosphere of warmth and understanding and an absence of indifference or irritation. It may be expressed in a smile, an understanding nod, or a hand on one's shoulder; indeed, if we had to sum it up in one word, that word would be 'love'. In an accepting environment a person will feel safe and secure and will be able to express himself openly. Through this absence of a fear of losing love the process of being open to all kinds of experiences can be optimal. This is the ideal situation for the development of the individual.

The origin of problems

How do personal problems arise? Once again Rogers believes that the person's environment has considerable influence. As the converse of 'unconditional regard' he introduces the concept of 'conditional regard'. This conditional type of care and attention is found when the person's environment no longer accepts him the way he is but instead makes love and acceptance dependent on him behaving in other, 'better' ways. As a result the person is forced to behave in ways contrary to how he really wants in order to secure the love, care, and attention so necessary to his feelings of safety and well-being. However, the 'price' he has to pay for this is that he is no longer free and spontaneous in the way he acts. The stricter the conditions placed on acceptance and the more these conditions deviate from his own tendencies and behaviour, the more this person will get into - difficulties.

In order to indicate the difference between 'being' and 'having to be' (in order to gain acceptance), Rogers introduces the term 'incongruence'. A person is in a state of incongruence when he no longer dares to act according to his own intuition and judgement but starts to conform in his behaviour and actions to the norms of his environment. It is important to note that the person does not choose this as an alternative to make his situation more bearable but because he has internalized the messages of how he should behave.

This process of internalization of imposed norms makes a person confused and anxious. It is difficult for him to follow his own judgement and he feels a continual conflict of feelings and thoughts between his own standards and those sanctioned by his environment. He becomes cautious about displaying his real self as he has internalized feelings that he is a failure and tries to cover up what he views as his shortcomings.

Rogers' method

The state of incongruence described in the previous section will probably be familiar to most of us. This is not surprising as we are talking about ordinary people with problems and there are few people who go through life without problems. The state of perfect congruence and self-actualization is an ideal which we can only strive towards. That we have not attained the ideal does not immediately mark us out as people with serious problems, it is obviously a matter of degree.

In the light of Rogers' belief in the importance of unconditional positive regard, what does this imply about how we should act in helping clients to solve their problems? The overall answer to this is evidently that we should behave towards the client in ways to compensate for the behaviour of important people in the client's environment which acts to impede the self-actualization process. Rogers has much to say about how this may be achieved in practice.

Unconditional positive regard

In order for the helper to show unconditional positive regard he will have to accept the client the way he is, warts and all. He will have to accept behaviours, opinions, and feelings that he may not himself agree with. This implies respect for the client and a recognition of his right to do the things and hold the opinions that he does. This does not mean that the helper should condone everything the client does or thinks but it does mean that he accepts the client's special individual qualities without judging or condemning him.

Genuineness

A second condition made by Rogers is that the helper should be 'genuine' in his relation with the client which means that he should function in an authentic, congruent, and integrated manner. It is of prime importance that the helper is honest and true to himself. This entails that the helper may allow himself all kinds of thoughts and feelings regarding the client, including some less generous or complimentary ones. Thus he may think to himself, 'This man is disgustingly fat', or, 'I am afraid of this woman'. 'Genuineness', however, should not be allowed to lead to a kind of thoughtless spontaneity with the counsellor saying straight out to the client, 'I think you are disgustingly fat', or, 'I am afraid of you!' The point is that the helper should acknowledge all his feelings about the client and use them appropriately during the counselling contact. In short, the helper in his relation with the client should first of all be able to accept his own thoughts and feelings.

According to Rogers, the helper need not always be perfectly congruent and integrated in his everyday life. He does, however, emphasize that the helper should strive for genuineness during his time with the client. Only by recognizing and acknowledging one's own thoughts and feelings can one hope to function in a way that may help a client gain a perspective on his thoughts and feelings.

Empathy

When the helper can accept the client unconditionally and acts towards him in a genuine manner it is possible for him to enter, without distortion, the client's private world of experience. This capacity for experiencing the client's perspective as if it were your own, without, however, losing sight of the 'as if' quality, is termed empathy by Rogers. He writes:

> To sense the client's private world as if it were your own, but without ever losing the 'as if' quality – this is empathy and this seems essential to therapy. To sense the client's anger, fear, or confusion as if it were your own, yet without your own anger, fear, or confusion getting bound up in it, is the condition we are endeavouring to describe.
>
> (Rogers 1957: 99)

However, experiencing the client's world is not enough. We must make him perceive that we feel and appreciate what he is going through. For this we need to be able to express ourselves in such a way that he recognizes that we understand him. This expression does not have to be purely verbal: non-verbal forms of communication such as gesture, posture, or facial expression may be very effective in helping to show that we comprehend the client's situation. We will discuss such factors in more detail in Chapter 6.

Empathy is of such importance for a number of reasons. First, it contributes to the client's feeling of security in his contact with the counsellor. What it expresses is the helper showing: 'I really want to understand you and feel what is going through your mind, and whatever it is I won't condemn you for it. My only concern is with the way you really are.' To a client who has been subjected to conditional regard this is a new, pleasant, and perhaps strange experience. 'The counsellor understands me and still feels I'm worthwhile enough that he wants to help me!' The client feels that he can be himself and does not have to pretend to be someone he is not. This freedom and security can by itself give the client space to begin to sort out his thoughts and feelings. The counsellor's unwillingness to judge or condemn is one of the most characteristic aspects of the client-centred approach advocated by Rogers. In certain respects, of course, all types of counselling may be said to be 'centred' around the client. Rogers uses the term 'client-centred' because of his belief that the helper should as far as possible aim to enter the client's experiential world and trust the client to find for himself the most appropriate solutions to his problems. Hence the approach is client-centred in that at no point does the counsellor try to impose his own standards on the client by judging or criticizing him.

However, an empathic response to be effective involves more than mere reflection of the client's experience. Rogers states:

> When the client's world is clear to the counselor and he can move about in it freely, then he can both communicate his understanding of what is vaguely known to the client, and he can also voice meanings in the client's experience of which the client is scarcely aware. It is this kind of highly sensitive empathy which seems important in making it possible for a person to get close to himself and to learn, to change and develop.
>
> (Rogers 1962: 420)

From this extract we can see that once the helper has really put himself in the client's place he can do more in his reactions than just reproduce the client's thoughts and feelings. 'He can also voice meanings in the client's experience of which the client is only scarcely aware.' This does not entail a distanced, intellectualized description of the client's thoughts and feelings but should rather closely reflect the client's experience so that he is prompted to remark, 'Yes, that's just it', or, 'Yes that's exactly how I feel'. The new perceptions that this use of empathy may engender may cause the client to start thinking about his problems in a different, more productive way.

It is a widespread misconception about empathy that the empathic counsellor need not do anything apart from 'mirroring', reflecting the thoughts expressed by the client back to him in exactly the same form. We have seen that the counsellor working with true empathy certainly does not act like a parrot and that there is a high degree of sophistication in his responses. Furthermore, the skilled helper will tailor his approach according to the stage of counselling; thus he will generally make increased use of reflected meaning as counselling progresses. We will return to this point when we come to discuss Wexler's theory later in this chapter.

A second misunderstanding about Rogers' ideas concerns the concept of 'non-directiveness'. This concept has often been interpreted very literally and viewed as characteristic of the client-centred approach. However, non-directiveness does not exist in reality. Even in an encounter where one has the aim of being consistently empathic it is impossible to react to everything that the client says in exactly the same way. Consciously or unconsciously the helper is bound to respond to some aspects more empathically than to others, and to this extent the counsellor manages the interview and determines the nature and direction of the discussion.

While Rogers claims to be non-directive in his interviewing style there is evidence that his own general orientation does have an effect on the course of sessions. Research (Truax 1966) shows that there is a demonstrable relationship between the nature of the client's utterances and the nature and intensity of the helper's reactions. Rogers himself was found to react more empathically and with greater warmth as his client's statements became more personal and showed a higher degree of self-perception. Conversely, he proved to be less empathic and accepting as client's statements became vaguer and more ambitious. Thus it would seem that Rogers was directing his clients to discuss their problems in a particular way. It is, therefore, clear that we need to be extremely careful in guarding against influencing the client, and in order to do this we need to monitor our reactions very closely.

In our view, the above discussion makes it clear that Rogers' theory is not sufficient by itself in directing the counsellor's technique. We therefore need theories which give the counsellor insight into patterns of dysfunctional thinking and behaviour and how to correct these (Trower, Casey, and Dryden 1988). In the next section we will first provide a more comprehensive critique of Rogers' theory before discussing how it might be supplemented by other theories.

A critique of Rogers' theory

Rogers' theory and methods have found widespread acclaim. His positive image of man, his belief in the potential for personal development, and his respect for personal choice have found a response in all those who have sought to reject the frequently paternalistic attitude found in much of the helping literature. However, in recent years well-founded criticism of Rogers' views has led to the development of new trends. We will discuss the most relevant of these points of criticism and then discuss our own perspective, including the theoretical basis within which we will propose supplements to Rogers' basic theory.

Is Rogers too optimistic?

Rogers' basic concept that a person has a potential for self-actualization which under favourable circumstances develops naturally is believed by many psychologists (particularly those of the behaviourist school) to be too optimistic. Thus behaviourists state that processes of self-actualization do not take place by themselves, they only occur when the person is reinforced for appropriate behaviours. They stress that a person should be reinforced and corrected in his learning process (Skinner 1948, 1953). When the environment does not provide such reinforcers self-actualization does not ensue. So there is more at stake than unconditional positive regard only. Furthermore, Rogers has been criticized for being too optimistic in describing the range of applicability of his theory and methods. His way of working requires that the client should be capable of thinking through his problems, of putting his thoughts and feelings into words, and of using his insight to formulate appropriate plans of action. All of these tasks require a relatively high level of intellectual development and functioning in addition to a certain degree of verbal fluency and dexterity. Goldstein (1973) has discovered that for large parts of the population whose abilities lie elsewhere Rogers' methods are difficult to apply. What these people require are more concrete methods which teach them how to solve their problems. Understanding and insight are still essential but they are not sufficient on their own.

Behaviourist theory raises another objection to Rogers' perspective which concerns his concept of self-actualization arising as a consequence of man's innate 'goodness'. How are we to understand this 'goodness'? Rogers seems to believe 'goodness' to be an inherent quality of all human beings. However, 'good' is surely a norm determined by the particular culture and 'good' acts result from an interaction between the person's personality and his environment. From this viewpoint it is not enough just to leave the person room for his own development. While warmth and understanding are essential in the helping relationship the helper must also be able to act as a stimulus for change. It is often necessary for the helper to point out the negative consequences of the client's actions and to emphasize his responsibility for them. As part of this, the client's obligations to others must be discussed and the fact demonstrated that life is a matter of give and take. Part of this process is implicit in the setting of conditions for helping which the counsellor carries out in consultation with the client. To be confronted with a 'taking' helper who makes demands can be very educational for a client who is used to receiving but not giving. As early as the 1960s it was discovered that Rogerian counsellors were inclined to support the client in whatever demands he made but neglected to emphasize the client's obligations to others (Brayfield 1962). By acting in this way it is questionable to what extent they were really helping their clients.

Is Rogers' theory too vague?

The 1970s saw a great expansion in the field of cognitive psychology. Cognitive psychology concerns itself with the way in which a person selects, codes, and stores information and makes it available for later use. This information processing enables the person to make sense of a seemingly endless stream of information. However, the meaning that people ascribe to events may be influenced in a number of ways. The solution to many problems may be sought in a deliberate adjustment of the style of information processing (a process sometimes termed cognitive reconstruction). Counselling methods based on this approach pay considerable attention to involving the client in modifying his information processing. Thus the client is viewed as being able to learn ways of altering his thinking patterns and of thereby gaining insight into and control over his own functioning.

One objection to Rogers' theory made by the cognitive school concerns the lack of directivity in its approach, particularly in its insufficient influence in modifying cognitive processes (Ellis 1974). According to the cognitive perspective such influence should take the form of pointing out to the client his erroneous and confused ways of thinking and of proposing alternatives, perhaps followed by training to improve skills of thinking and acting.

A second criticism is that Rogers' theory is unclear about the way in which a process of self-actualization is brought about. In particular the assertion that such a process takes place naturally provided that the person is 'open' to his experiences seems very vague. Cognitive psychologists have been particularly critical of the concept of a natural self-actualization process and in a later section we will look at an alternative perspective proposed by Wexler.

Is Rogers' theory really essential?

Although we agree with many of the criticisms of Rogers' *theory*, we believe that his *method* has many assets and we would argue that it is possible to subscribe to the main principles of his methods without necessarily agreeing with his theory of human development. Patterson (1986) has reviewed a range of personality theories and the psychotherapies based on them and discusses points on which there seems to be a general consensus in counselling. Most importantly, all schools of counselling seem to agree on the need for a good relationship between helper and client (in the Rogerian sense) as a condition for efficient helping. Hence it is essential that the helper should have good interpersonal skills. The effect of a close and genuine relationship between helper and client goes beyond simply building up a firm basis for cooperation. Many clients have had a history of bad experiences in personal relationships. The warm and uncritical nature of the contact with the counsellor may be a revelation for them, an example which influences their own behaviour and enhances their relationships with others around them.

In the introduction to this chapter we briefly commented on the range of applicability of various counselling theories and methods. Rogers' techniques give the client the opportunity to discover solutions to his problems as independently as possible. When it is only necessary for the helper to offer understanding and security he should do no more. The more he does the greater the chance that he does something wrong. Helping people is a complicated and risky undertaking and Rogers' main theme is that helpers should interfere as little as is necessary. In this sense his views are still essential for counselling.

A cognitive theory of experiencing

From our discussion so far it has become obvious that a client-centred helper is not non-directive and that in his empathic reactions he does more than just showing the client that he appreciates his experiences. We have noted that effective helpers do something extra to help the client further with his problems. However, this leaves us with a number of questions. What is this 'extra'? How does the helper put it into practice? When is it to be used appropriately? How does its use fit in with the 'development' of the person as conceptualized by Rogers? These are difficult questions and to throw some light on them we will discuss personal functioning from the perspective of cognitive psychology. In doing this we will draw extensively on the work of Wexler (1974), an information theorist of the client-centred school. We will give a brief outline of his theory and discuss how its insights can be used in a modification of Rogers' theory which answers some of the criticisms mentioned earlier in this chapter.

Experiencing as an active process

Let us summarize: in Rogers' theory a person is viewed as having a potential for self-actualization which is achievable through changes in the quality of his experiencing. The process of self-actualization can be disturbed by external influences such as the quality of interpersonal relationships. It is the counsellor's task to promote the self-actualization tendency by creating a climate of security by way of the conditions described on pp. 27–30. The client then becomes more open to his own experiences and feelings because he no longer has to be on his guard about what he should or should not say, think, feel, etc. Under these conditions the client can achieve his full potential. The question now becomes: how does this happen, what does the client do himself, and which potential is realized? Rogers is very vague about this. His work encourages the metaphor of a plant which with light, water, and the right nutrients grows naturally into what it should ideally become. However, does a person 'grow' in the same way?

Wexler has a number of comments to make about this point. Like

Rogers he believes in a process of self-actualization but differs from Rogers in the *way* in which he sees the process taking place.

Rogers believes that in order to experience fully it is sufficient to open oneself to impressions from inside and outside. From this perspective experiencing seems to be a *passive* process. It appears that the person must surrender to external and internal stimuli.

Wexler rejects this notion of a passive form of experiencing and, drawing on research into perceptual processes and information processing, points out that we experience our world in an active way. Far from being passive and receptive to every stimulus, leading to an overwhelming intake of information, man is active in selecting, arranging, and bestowing meaning on his impressions. It is of vital importance for a person to be selective and discriminating in dealing with the large quantity of information directed at him. In our everyday lives we all recognize that we can only absorb a limited amount of stimuli and that we are not truly receptive to all the stimuli occurring in our environment. Thus when a person is listening to music he does not hear flies buzzing around him. He does not see much of what is going on around him and he may even close his eyes in order to concentrate better on the music. However, surely Rogers recognizes this as well? Certainly his concept of 'being open to experience' is not meant as passively as Wexler takes it and we will discuss exactly what Rogers' concept entails on p. 40.

We have seen that information processing is an active mental process in which a person 'digests' his experiences. Everyone has his own way of doing this. Not only does everyone select information in his own way, but the interpretation of this information also takes place in an idiosyncratic fashion: 'things do not have meaning *in* them: people bestow meaning *on* them' (Wexler 1974: 57). An example makes this point more clearly.

Client: My wife does not love me any more.
Helper: What makes you say that? Can you give me an example?
Client: Some time ago I went to see the doctor. My wife waited for me in the car and when I came out I told her I was very ill and had to go into hospital. I was very upset. At first she was quiet and then she said, 'We must hurry to do the shopping, the shops will soon be shut.' I ask you!

It seems that it has not occurred to the client that his wife's way of reacting may have reflected her shock and anxiety at news which she could not deal with adequately at that very moment, precisely because of her love for him. Therefore she reacted in this blunt manner. In everyday language we have a number of ways of expressing differences in interpretation: 'I look at it differently', 'I understand it differently', etc. This shows that people can order and interpret the same basic information in different ways. Thus one can learn to change the meaning that is placed on a particular event and when, in our example, the helper gives the alternative interpretation of the wife's behaviour, the client might say, 'Oh yes, that might be right, I haven't looked at it that way.' This might be an important discovery for the client and lead him to start thinking about other events in a different manner. Everyone has learnt to interpret information in his own idiosyncratic fashion although we are not always aware of this. Often it is only noticed when others see the same facts differently.

The processing of information is a fairly complicated procedure which we will not go into in detail. However, some of its features are important for a full understanding of the counselling process. First, it is necessary to recognize the crucial part that language plays in information processing. To be able to put feelings into words allows us to understand them better. To be able to label our experiences and to discuss them helps us to make sense of our everyday lives. When people have problems, talking about them often clarifies the situation: 'Let me talk about it and try to get things straight in my mind.' Often this new clarity is not agreeable, the seriousness of the problem may become more apparent, making us more sharply aware that something is wrong.

A second feature of information processing concerns two complementary processes: differentiation and integration. Differentiation describes the process by which we refine our beliefs and attitudes on the basis of incoming information. Let us consider a person who believes 'All Scotsmen are tight-fisted' who encounters a Scotsman throwing his money about. The person's image of Scotsmen may then become more differentiated: 'So there are some mean Scotsmen, and some generous ones.' His belief system has been enriched, with more nuances. The same phenomenon may occur with the experiencing of internal processes. A client states, 'I feel so alone.' This might mean a range of things. By talking further he may become more aware of the background to the feeling, for instance by realizing that it signifies to him: 'Nobody cares about me' but also 'I feel particularly lonely when I spend a weekend at home alone.' By talking and thinking through what the feeling really consists of he acquires a better insight into his emotions instead of the previous confused, all-embracing feeling of loneliness.

Integration describes the process by which connections are made between different pieces of information, and an overall pattern is discovered. A whole is made from the constituent parts and an orderly view of the world is maintained. Integration enriches our experience by allowing us to make sense of disparate pieces of information and to make predictions for the future. In short, through differentiation, a number of refinements are made to people's way of experiencing the world, while through integration connections are made and an overall view is obtained. This active process of continual differentiation and integration allows us to assimilate fully new information, giving it structure and meaning.

What relevance do these processes of differentiation and integration have for work with clients? Ideally the processes run smoothly and the person has rules and methods which allow him to deal with conflicting information. However, when the processes can no longer cope with incoming information the person has difficulties in making sense of his experiences. He cannot come to 'grips' with them and problems are likely to result. In such cases the helper's task is clear: he must help the client to order his information differently so that he experiences the world in a more controllable way. We will discuss how the helper may achieve this in a later section.

The role of feelings

It is probable that many readers have become a little disappointed with the purely intellectual approach to helping that we have so far described: shouldn't feelings be involved as well? Indeed they should, although in Wexler's view they occupy a different place of importance than in Rogers' perspective. We would like to make some comments on this subject but would point out that in the space available we do not claim to do justice to the whole complexity of the field of emotional experiences (Frijda 1986).

In Rogers' theory feelings play an essential part. To experience emotions, to be open to them, is of prime importance. It makes it possible to live as an individual, recognizing and accepting one's own emotions. While Wexler accepts Rogers' belief in the importance of fully experiencing emotions, he points out that the latter's theory does not make it clear how such emotions arise in the first place. Rogers seems to imply that feelings are stored somewhere in ourselves and emerge when we are open to them, which means that they automatically come to the fore. Wexler, however, stresses that emotions do not occur by themselves but are directly linked to cognitive processes. In his view feelings occur as a result of information processing. In the preceding section we noted that the processing of information is an active process.

> Rather than seeing change as *resulting* from an 'intensive, affective or feeling process', the present view sees affect as *produced* by the activity of processing substantive information. Affect in therapy is a by-product of the client's activity of distinguishing and synthesizing facets of meaning that create reorganization and change in the field.
>
> (Wexler 1974: 81)

The question which now arises is why the processing of information is sometimes linked to feelings and at other times is not. Wexler mentions several factors to account for this. First, the significance of the information for the person involved will have an important influence. Chatting about the weather, even when it contains new information, will not move us to tears. With personal information, however, there is a much greater likelihood that there will be an emotional reaction. Nevertheless, the significance of the subject is not sufficient in itself to predict the emotional outcome. For instance, some people are capable of talking quite unemotionally about their marriage or future career plans.

Another factor involved in the occurrence of emotions is the degree to which the person's world is in a state of change. Thus people may experience a wide range of strong emotions when a disorganization occurs in their system of information processing, with new information being added which does not fit into the existing structure but which nevertheless has to be accommodated. Sudden changes – failure to pass an exam, being made redundant, etc. – cause confusion in the person's system and result in feelings of insecurity and anxiety. Once the information is incorporated these feelings of anxiety are replaced by other feelings. The duration of this process will vary considerably depending on a number of factors including the nature of the change, its significance for the person, and the person's previous experience of similar changes.

A third circumstance in which it is likely that information processing will result in an emotional reaction occurs when new information causes the person to re-examine their previously held beliefs
and opinions. Recalling the client from the previous example who
believed his wife did not love him, we may note how he reviewed his
belief when the helper showed him alternative interpretations for his
wife's reactions. His new thought 'Perhaps she does still love me
after all!' will evidently promote new emotions, perhaps of surprise
and joy.

With the above examples we hope to have demonstrated Wexler's
view that the crucial point in the arousal of emotions is the processing of certain types of information.

The view described above of the relationship between some aspects of information processing and emotions has important consequences when working with clients. In counselling, significant
changes which are beneficial to the client are often accompanied by
strong emotions. However, from this we should not conclude that in
order to effect significant change it is necessary to evoke strong feelings in the client: an 'appeal to sentiment' should not become an end
in itself. When the client does display strong emotions it can be
taken by the helper as an indication to watch out carefully for
changes in the client and to clarify what is happening to him. Naturally the helper should also accept and aim to understand these feelings so that the client feels free to experience and express them.
However, the helper is also responsible for ensuring that things do
not get out of hand. Anxiety, confusion, depression, etc. should not
be stimulated to such a degree that the client's distress becomes des-
pair and hopelessness. It is the helper's task to assist the client in
such a way that he does not go home completely overwrought or confused.

We believe that a warning should be given to those who, particularly in training and other group activities, believe in evoking all
kinds of strong emotions in participants by creating unexpected situations, setting new standards, or by the use of an authoritarian
leadership style. This is often defended by the argument that strong
feelings in the group setting provoke powerful reactions and that the
group members are sure to make 'progress' in this way. In some cases
this method may prove successful but in our view the risk is very
great that participants will actually end up further away from achieving their goals (Koch 1971).

Does Rogers really regard experiencing as passive?

On p. 35 we briefly noted that Wexler's criticism of Rogers for viewing experiences as a passive process was to a large extent unjustified and based on a too literal reading of his work. In our view Wexler does Rogers an injustice by suggesting that the latter states that the person should be passively open to experience in order to feel more intensely. Rogers 'asks' the person to pay more attention to emotions and suggests that such emotions should be recognized as information which needs to be processed so that it can be given its true value. This is a form of actively directing one's attention. When the client does not process certain information, in this case does not pay attention to inner feelings and dismisses them because it has been learnt that expressing feelings is taboo, the experiencing process is impoverished. In these situations Rogers will subtly stimulate the client to pay attention to his emotions and to put them into words so that they may be processed more effectively. This is precisely what Wexler means by 'selection of information'.

We do not want to diminish the value of Wexler's contribution and his recognition of the person as an active processor of information. Importantly, he emphasizes that the counselling enterprise should not be allowed to degenerate into an excessive emphasis on just feelings allowing the client to 'drown' in a 'sea' of emotions. Our reanalysis of Rogers' theory to modify Wexler's views is intended to underline that the processing of information should not be viewed as a purely active process but as a dynamic balance between active agency and a more passive 'openness' to experience. We see here the necessity for equilibrium: between intellect and sentiment, between action and receptivity.

Chapter four

The social learning approach

Introduction

In the last chapter we discussed human information processing and noted how every individual learns his own way of making sense of his experiences. We now need to look more closely at how this learning process takes place.

One of the points on which Rogers' theory was criticized in the previous chapter was his optimistic view that a person's development arises naturally as long as circumstances promote sufficient freedom and space. His emphasis is on growth rather than on learning. Wexler's cognitive theory tells part of the story of how we learn to give meaning to our experiences. According to him a person 'makes' his own world through a process of selection, differentiation, and integration of incoming information. He points out the importance of learning to process information in a different way in order to give a more adaptive perspective on personal problems. However, this still leaves out of account another important part of the story, that to overcome their problems people also have to learn to *act* differently, to behave in other ways. Social learning theory provides a framework for understanding how learning processes result in changes in thinking and doing. Humans are conceptualized as being learning creatures influenced by their environment but also themselves shaping it. In the following discussion we draw on the work of Bandura (1977, 1986) and Mischel (1968, 1973).

We will first discuss the image of the person inherent in social learning theory. We will then consider principles involved in the learning of behaviour and self-control. Finally, we describe a common pattern of problems which result from the person setting unrealistic goals and ideals.

The social learning perspective

Social learning theory describes humans as creatures with enormous potential for development. This potential operates within biologically determined boundaries and in a complicated interaction with influences from the environment. This interaction is expressed by Bandura (1977) in the formula:

By person (P) is meant the collection of traits, styles of thinking and doing, and other personal characteristics. We have in mind biographical data such as sex, age, marital status, race, religion, education, and so on. Hereditary traits such as hair colour, quickness of reaction, physical strength, intellectual capacities, etc. also belong to this category. From this enumeration can be deduced that it is not only a question of purely hereditary or biological characteristics. Also included are more or less durable traits, developed (further) under the influence of growing and learning processes. With behaviour (B) we indicate the actual observable behaviour in various situations. By environment (E) we mean a multitude of situations, consisting of other persons who knowingly or not influence P and B. We will demonstrate the mutual influencing of P, E, and B with some examples.

When a person is solving crossword puzzles the degree to which he is able to do so (B) depends largely on intellectual factors (P→B). To do this often (B), however, results in experience which in general increases the capacity for solving puzzles and hence will lead to self-confidence (P) in dealing with this kind of problem (B→P). When the environment, for example the family, thinks the solving of crossword puzzles is important, the person will think so as well (E→P), so that this behaviour will be stimulated (E→B). Conversely a skilful crossword puzzler will influence his environment; his assistance is asked with difficult words (P→E) and he is admired for his quick solutions (B→E). This might stimulate him to go on practising and to become even more proficient (E→B→P).

By stating that B, P, and E function in a complicated process of mutual influencing we do not want to say that all three factors have equal influence. The relative influence may vary per person and/or per situation. Sometimes the environment will have an all-determining influence. A violent hailstorm (E) will cause everybody to seek shelter (B). Few people will by throwing back the hailstones (B) try to influence the environment (E)! Most persons have learned that this does not help at all. Sometimes the person is of considerable influence: a dominant personality (P) will bend the course of events in a meeting (E) to his will (P→E). We have deliberately chosen simple examples here. But we all know that in everyday life a multiform process of interactions is going on that has a considerable effect on all the three factors discussed here.

This means that when one is helping someone with his problems it is not enough to consider solely either his behaviour, his traits or his situation. Human behaviour is influenced by all these factors. Thus social learning theory demonstrates that to understand human functioning we must investigate it from a number of angles.

How is behaviour learnt?

The learning process is a complicated subject which has been investigated and described by a wide range of authors. In the framework of this book we will limit ourselves to the more important principles of social learning theory which have relevance to working with clients. In this discussion we will also show how learning is linked with other functions of the human organism such as perception, thinking, and motivation. We first discuss some general learning principles and then elaborate on these by considering the influence of external factors. In the next section we outline how the person influences his own behaviour through the setting of goals and plans. Finally we consider an example of excessive self-regulation resulting in personal problems.

Learning through modelling

We first learn most activities in life by watching others do them. In the scientific literature this is called 'modelling'. The term 'social learning theory' is derived from this emphasis on learning from the example of other people. To observe others offers the opportunity to learn new behaviour without the necessity of having to make embarrassing or possibly painful mistakes as part of the learning process. It is important to recognize that this learning from a model does not just apply to actions but also to thinking in so far as one can get to know about others' cognitive processes through their 'thinking aloud' in talking or writing.

By watching others in action people gain information on how certain activities are performed. Sooner or later they will then use that information as a basis for acting in a similar way themselves. This account of how people learn from models emphasizes the cognitive processes involved. Thus information is processed by the person in his own idiosyncratic way, is stored in memory, and can be retrieved at a later date.

For learning from a model to be effective a number of conditions must be met. First, the person must direct his attention to the model's behaviour and should be in a position to observe the behaviour in close detail. That is to say, he should be able to focus on the essential points of the behaviour. This has important consequences for teachers and instructors trying to educate people in new skills. For effective teaching it is necessary for pupils to be directed to the core features of how to carry out the task in hand. Thus a driving instructor who does not demonstrate to his pupils such skills as changing gear and using the brakes will find them very slow in learning to control the car adequately.

How well someone directs and maintains his attention on the task to be learnt will depend to a very great degree on his motivation. If somebody badly wants to learn how to play snooker he will watch the style of a good snooker player very closely. The value of the behaviour to the person will obviously influence how much effort he will put into learning it.

A second factor which will determine how well a behaviour is learnt from a model is the degree to which the person can remember what he has observed. The model behaviour must be stored in memory in a symbolized form if it is to be put to use later. Generally this storing of information in memory will be enhanced if the person can verbalize to himself the component parts of the behaviour. Bandura (1977) discovered that people learning a skill were able to learn it much more quickly if they could say to themselves what exactly was involved than if they only watched without putting into words what they saw.

A third condition to be met for effective learning from models involves opportunities to perform the behaviour. Knowing in theory how a behaviour should be performed does not necessarily mean that one can actually do it. Between knowing about it and being able to do it lies a world of difference. In many cases knowledge alone is not sufficient. Particularly where complex tasks are concerned it is doubtful whether one can acquire the necessary skills by observation alone. The transfer of knowledge into action requires practice. Often in carrying out such practice the person realizes that he is still not sure of all the details of the task and may need to gain some additional information.

The shaping of knowledge into action needs less practice if the new behaviour can be built up from skills that have already been learnt in another context. Thus the most effective way to explain to the boss why you deserve a raise may be easier to learn if you have previously gained good assertiveness skills in other circumstances, for example, from working in a union. It is then just a matter of refining certain details.

Learning by example is a very important way in which new behaviours are acquired. However, we have seen that for such learning to be effective certain conditions must be fulfilled. It is important for counsellors to realize this and to ensure that such conditions are met in all cases where the client is to learn a new skill. When they are not met, for example, by the client not attending to modelled behaviour or not having the chance to practise skills, the helping process may get stuck with insights not being translated into concrete actions. The result will very soon be a frustrated helper facing a frustrated client.

Learning through the consequences of actions

The learning of various behaviours is profoundly influenced by the consequences, positive or negative, of those behaviours. Thus behaviour which is followed by positive consequences is strengthened and is likely to be repeated by the person in comparable situations. Behaviour which is followed by negative consequences is more likely to be avoided in the future.

Learning from consequences is generally a conscious process whereby we recognize and contemplate the consequences of previous actions in deciding plans for the future. However, in many areas learning is more automatic, with less consideration of the outcome of a particular behaviour but with an internalized recognition of what the consequences are likely to be if the behaviour is repeated. Thus if we touch the hot-plate of a cooker and burn our hand it is not necessary for us to think about this incident in great detail for us to learn not to touch the hot-plate again!

When, in the course of counselling a client, it becomes clear that some behaviour needs to be changed, the consequence of that behaviour needs to be thoroughly investigated. Generally cognitive processes will play an important part in how a person interprets the outcomes of his actions. Thus it is people's interpretations of what happens (after they acted in a particular way) rather than what actually happens which will affect whether they act in the same way again. For example, if a person walks into a party and everybody turns to look at him he may interpret this event in a number of ways ranging from very positive to very negative. If he believes that people are looking at him because he is so handsome and smartly dressed he is likely to feel confident at the party and look forward to future parties. If, however, he interprets the stares as expressing disapproval or disgust he is likely to feel inhibited at the party and may prefer to avoid similar social occasions in the future. This demonstrates once more the important point that in dealing with clients helpers must appreciate that facts do not speak for themselves but rather it is the client's interpretation of the facts which is crucial.

The consequences of actions can have both informing and motivating functions. When people can see which of their behaviours have positive and which have negative results, they have acquired knowledge which will help them to work out how to behave in future. However, it is important for the person to recognize which part of their behaviour brought about the consequence. Thus when a driver is stopped by a policeman but is not told what he did wrong the driver may find it difficult to know how he needs to change his driving to avoid being stopped again. This brings us to the second function of consequences, namely the motivating one. When it is known what the likely result of a particular action will be, one will be motivated to either repeat or avoid repeating the action on succeeding occasions. Furthermore, the motivation for a particular behaviour will change as the consequences of that behaviour change. Thus if our weekly wage were to be suddenly halved we would probably find that our motivation to work hard would be seriously affected!

The informative and motivational aspects of the consequences of behaviour have an important role in its regulation, and we will examine this further in the next section.

How is behaviour regulated?

We have discussed the ways in which people learn from models and how the consequences of behaviour affect learning processes. It has also been seen that this process does not run according to a simple model whereby certain external stimuli bring about specific reactions in a totally predictable way. There is a crucial intermediary between stimuli and reactions: the person as information processor.

The influence of expectations

In order to function effectively people need to be able to look ahead and predict the probable outcome of their actions. By doing this they attempt to make optimal use of their own abilities in achieving their goals, while avoiding risks which seem too great. A world in which we were unable to look into the future and make plans and predictions would be a very frightening and confusing one. Our expectations are thus extremely important in guiding how we live and act. These expectancies are learnt through a continuing process of interpreting the connections between various events and outcomes. Some expectancies will be produced as a result of one's own experiences, some from the experiences of others.

Although anticipating the possible consequences of one's actions has several obviously useful functions, in some cases it can become maladaptive. Forming expectancies on the basis of too little information may make us closed to further, contradictory information. Thus if new neighbours, on the day of moving in, react curtly to my friendly welcome, I may think, 'What snooty people! I'll keep myself to myself in future!' If I persist in this attitude I will never find out what the neighbours are really like after getting over the chaos of moving.

An understanding of avoidance behaviours is very important in the helping process. Some vulnerable people get into social difficulties quickly because after a few bad experiences they start to avoid making contact with others. We have already noted how social contacts are crucial in enriching and modifying our own repertoire of behaviours, and the person who begins to avoid involvement with other people will soon start to show deficits in his social skills. This may lead to a vicious circle whereby an avoidance of social contact leads to poorer interpersonal skills, which then influence the person to avoid social situations even more strongly, and so on.

Influencing expectations

In social learning theory the importance of feelings of control is emphasized. When someone performs in a way which shows that he is in control of the situation expectancies of future performances in such situations are likely to be optimistic. Bandura distinguishes between *'outcome expectations'* and *'efficacy expectations'*. Outcome expectations are the result of the people's beliefs that certain behaviours will in general result in particular outcomes. Efficacy expectations concern people's beliefs that they are capable of behaving in ways needed to achieve the desired outcomes. The distinction between the two types of expectation may be illustrated by the example of a person considering asking his boss for a rise. He may rightly believe that he has only to explain his expertise and his value for the firm after many years of good job-fulfilment for his boss to give him the rise. His outcome expectation is high. However, when he starts to think about putting the plan into action he begins to feel that he isn't confident and articulate enough to influence his boss. His efficacy expectation is low and he feels anxious and powerless. The fact that he knows what he should do but feels incapable of doing it may have a detrimental effect on his self-confidence which in turn may make future efficacy expectations even more negative.

Efficacy expectations can be influenced in a number of ways. Planning difficult tasks in a stepwise manner may prevent early failures and the build-up of associated negative expectations. Viewing a person perceived as being similar to themselves completing a certain action may make people more confident of their own ability to act effectively. The person's emotional state will affect his efficacy expectations. A depressed person is likely to have negative expectations of his performance in certain situations. In Chapter 8 we will discuss in detail how practical use of these ideas can be made in dealing with problems.

Self-regulation

So far in this chapter we have mainly dealt with the influence of external factors on the way we behave and think. However, it is not only the environment which determines our actions. We are not just leaves blown by the wind. Even in the face of considerable external pressure we are able to develop and maintain our own ways of doing and thinking. This individual way of acting demonstrates the person's characteristic and personal style.

The person's own ability to regulate his behaviour makes him less a slave to his environment. He sets his own standards for behaviour and has his own rules regarding reward and punishment. Thus one's actions are influenced both by external factors ('What is my environment doing to me?') and internal factors ('What am I doing to myself?'). In connection with helping people with problems it is important to understand how people can gain control over their own behaviour. We will now investigate the nature of this self-regulation in more detail.

Processes of self-regulation

Self-regulation refers to the process by which the person in pursuit of a self-generated goal will reward himself for reaching certain standards he has set and punish himself for not reaching them. For example, in writing a book an author may set himself the task of writing ten pages in a day and will reward himself with a stiff drink if he achieves this goal.

By specifying his own rewards the person enhances his self-motivation to carry out the behaviour. This may lead to the person being very persistent in pursuit of his goals. Often outsiders do not understand anything of all these exertions. The person may even gain the reputation for being stubborn and unyielding.

People vary greatly in the standards that they set themselves. Thus some golfers are happy just to get around the course while others set a much more exacting standard of achieving a certain score or breaking par. In this process of setting standards comparisons with others will be very influential. Without being able to compare your performance against others it is difficult to judge how satisfied you should be. However, there still remains the choice of who to compare yourself against. There are many activities where one compares oneself with groups of others (Festinger 1954a, 1954b). With school tests students compare themselves with others in their class, footballers compare themselves with others in their team, etc. One can also compare oneself with oneself. Performances achieved in the past may serve as a yardstick with which to assess present performances. However, in doing this the person must take matters as the aging process into consideration: in matters of personal fitness the older person may have to expect a decline and the challenge may lie in making this decline as slow as possible.

In judging whether one's performance deserves reward or punishment the significance put on the activity will evidently be of great importance. We may not be very impressed by winning a game of noughts and crosses with a young nephew but beating the club squash champion may be a cause for celebration.

The tyranny of the ideal-image

In previous sections we have stated that self-esteem is to a large extent determined by people comparing their own actions with those they look upon as being their ideal. The level of self-esteem depends mainly on the discrepancy between what has been achieved and what one wants to achieve. It will also be influenced by the degree to which this discrepancy is tolerated.

When people view their ideal as being within their capacity to achieve, the motivation to succeed may be high. The person sets his goals and strives with confidence to attain them. If the ideals are not achieved at the first attempt, as long as they are still perceived as being possible to achieve, the person will still be motivated and may even be encouraged to try harder.

A more difficult phenomenon, which can sometimes interfere with a person's happiness, is the image of an unattainable ideal. When a person has such an ideal he may place exhaustive demands on himself and become excessively self-critical. It often seems that our western society promotes such unattainable ideals and encourages people fanatically to seek goals of success and status which can never quite be achieved. Of course, we do not wish to advocate that people should not have goals, and people who work hard and are satisfied with their achievements receive our greatest admiration. However, we are more concerned that by setting too high an ideal image they may torment themselves, and by aiming at goals which cannot be reached end up with feelings of failure, powerlessness, guilt, and inferiority. A vicious circle may then ensue whereby these feelings lead to reduced self-confidence, resulting in a poorer performance and yet more self-reproach. In such situations people may still attempt to cling to their ideal in a number of ways: excessive daydreaming, phantasizing, telling 'tall' stories, etc. Alternatively they may place the blame for not achieving their goals on other people and become angry and critical towards family or friends. It can thus be seen that exaggerated ambitions and strict demands on oneself may change from being a positive, stimulating influence into a restraining or even destructive one.

It is often difficult for people to recognize that they have got into a cycle of endlessly chasing an impossible ideal. For many people it is natural to be hard on themselves and to take things any easier would be perceived as slacking. Even more difficult may be the admission that they are not achieving what they should and as a result feel a failure. The person who is brave enough to face up to how he is making himself dissatisfied by setting too high standards is taking an enormous step forward. After all, to acknowledge the need to set more realistic targets may entail an abandonment of some cherished dreams. To admit such matters to a helper requires a great deal of trust as from previous experiences the person may have come to expect punishment for any admissions of failure. As with a true friendship, a valuable aspect of the counselling relationship is that you are allowed to show yourself for what you are and then to find that you are still accepted, warts and all, and through this learn to accept yourself (Ellis 1974).

One reason for carefully assessing the influence of a strict ideal as part of the helping process is that a failure to recognize it may lead to the wrong approach being taken. This may be illustrated with an example.

A counsellor is visited by a nervous client. He is the teacher of a large class who wants to give more attention to his pupils and their problems. Aside from running a range of school-related activities he is also chairman of the local branch of a political party and a keen member of a squash club. He is dissatisfied with the way he talks with his pupils and feels that he is failing to help them with problems that they have. He therefore wants to learn from the helper how to improve his manner of dealing with the children and feels that he may also pick up something which might help to improve relations with his wife and children.

How does the helper approach this client's difficulties? Initially he will aim to promote a relaxed atmosphere in which he can find out more about the client's situation, his hopes and aspirations, and the demands that he makes on himself. In such a case we feel it is important that the helper should not start on any form of training programme too quickly. The helper may try to get the client to reinterpret his 'failure' as an achievement, for example as displaying his deep care and concern for his pupils. The client may thus come to realize that the reason for his unsatisfactory contacts with his pupils and his family may reflect his desire to do too well – the alternative is clear: to try less hard. The helper may even use the client's desire for achievement in a paradoxical way by encouraging him to work seriously on this 'doing less'.

Problems can be more complex than in the case above. Not only may discrepancies between the ideal and the actual situation vary widely, but also the importance attached to such discrepancies may differ. For example, a woman comes for counselling because she has marital difficulties. After a couple of sessions an overview of her situation is obtained.

She wants a very good relationship with her husband. The existing relationship, as she sees it, is not bad. So there is not a big distance between the ideal-image and the actual situation. However, although this distance is small, this is an area of prime importance to her and she therefore feels a strong need to improve the situation.

Though her relationship with her parents is unsatisfactory, her demands in this area are not very high. The distance between the actual situation and how it should be is considerable, but she says, 'They are quite different from me, I am a little worried about this but I do not blame myself too much.' Thus, although the distance is great, because this relationship is of minor importance to her, she is not too concerned.

She works as sales manager in a clothing store. In general she likes the work. Sometimes she has some trouble with the junior sales staff who in her opinion do not have their hearts in the business and are not attentive enough. She believes that she should act tough in those cases and see to it that the situation improves; she looks upon that as her duty but feels that she falls down badly in this objective. So there is a distance between the ideal-image and the actual situation. Sometimes she blames herself a lot, but at other times she takes the situation less seriously: 'Perhaps I am too strict in my demands of the other sales-persons and myself.' She also notices to her surprise that her more easygoing manner has a positive effect on the willingness of the staff to do a little extra.

What we aim to show by this example is that complex issues of self-image, ideal-image, and self-esteem can be analysed systematically in individual cases. When the differences between self- and ideal-image are large in a wide range of the person's areas of functioning, self-reproach may generalize and an accelerating process of depression may result.

It is not always easy to decide which problem to tackle first. It is a matter of discussion between helper and client as to which are the main priorities and which are the easier difficulties to concentrate on. They will then decide to address a high priority area which is also likely to be reasonably easy to resolve given the client's present level of confidence and ability.

Finally, we can place the information obtained by the helper within the context of the client's personal history. This can often be very enlightening. In our previous example this may result in questions such as: 'How much did you bother about the relationship with your parents in the past?' The reply might be: 'Well, I used to be worried about it but I'm not so concerned about it these days as I have less contact with them anyway.' Such answers give information which the helper can use to help the client appreciate her capacity to deal with other situations. If the client recognizes how, through her efforts, certain areas of her life are more satisfactory than they were previously she may feel much more confident that she will achieve success in tackling other areas.

We have combined several aspects of the theories outlined so far with some relevant practical methods. This forms a bridge to the following chapters where we shall consider in depth the tasks of the helper in the helping process.

Chapter five

The helper at work

Introduction

The theories discussed in Chapters 3 and 4 were chosen to support the helper's work in practice. They give guidelines for structuring his actions. But theories alone are not enough. The helper must set himself a definite *goal*. He will then have to choose a fitting *role*, that is, an approach suited to the goal to be reached. And in order to maintain an overall view of the goals and the roles during counselling, he will need a *helping model*. This chapter deals with these three subjects.

Clarity of goals

We all know from daily experience how a conversation, certainly when touching on emotional subjects, tends to skip from one topic to another. After a while the starting point is often lost: 'What exactly were we talking about?' For daily use such a rambling conversation does not matter much. In counselling, however, things are different. The purpose of such a counselling session is obvious: to reduce personal problems. If the helper wants to reach this goal, the interview should follow a more or less orderly course. The helper is the person primarily responsible, even in a cooperative model, for an orderly course of the conversation. In order to know whether a conversation is going well, both helper and client should have a goal in mind. Only when they have set themselves definite goals will they be able to find out whether their interaction has helped to reach that goal.

But how can we formulate goals when this is just what we would like the client to do himself? And how can we set these goals when the problems are still vague? We shall now elaborate on the concept of a goal.

When a client goes to a helper because 'something' is bothering him, he almost certainly has as a goal the reduction or even solution of this problematic 'something'. We find that the beginning of a counselling session is often vague in this way. One may wonder what is the point of setting goals at such an early stage when the helper is still in the dark; would it not be better to let the client continue exploring for a while? That is true, but then for the time being this is the goal of the counsellor.

It is useful at this point to distinguish between various types of goal during counselling. There is a considerable difference between goals relating to the helping process and goals relating to the outcome, the intended outcome of giving help (Hackney and Cormier 1979). The helper uses *process goals* to create the right conditions for effective counselling. One such process goal, for instance, is the creation of an atmosphere of calm and trust at the beginning of the interview. The process goals are the means selected by the helper to reach outcome goals. On the basis of this description it is clear that selecting process goals and searching for methods and techniques to reach them, are mainly the responsibility of the helper.

At the beginning of a first counselling contact the process goals will be more or less the same for each client. The helper does not know anything yet. The client comes to him to talk and the goal of the helper should be to create favourable conditions for talking: 'Let me first listen quietly, I can do no more at this stage.' By explicitly setting himself this goal, the helper also promotes a certain calm in himself; he is not obliged to do anything further yet. As the interview progresses, the helper will wonder which direction he wants the interview to take. The choice of process goals is determined more and more by the insight he gains into the problems and the behaviour of the client.

As the contact with the client progresses, defining the process goals becomes not necessarily the responsibility of the helper alone. He can involve the client in his plans. He can explain, for example, that in order to find a reachable goal, it is necessary to discuss the client's problems as concretely as possible and ask him to cooperate in this.

The outcome goals – the second type – are different for each client, since personal problems of each individual usually require a tailor-made solution. So the choice of outcome goals is mainly the responsibility of the client. As discussed in Chapter 2, we think that the client should choose for himself how he wants to shape his life. This implies that the choice of a solution for a problem in his life is his own affair. Looking for acceptable outcome goals and finding ways to achieve them is a joint undertaking of helper and client. The client should look upon the goal as his goal, so as to ensure that he is motivated to reach it.

Helper and client need to be flexible in choosing and, if necessary, changing their process and outcome goals. When the contact with the helper has just started, the problems are often rather vague, so that only general goals can be aimed at. Nevertheless, helper and client need these goals to give some direction to their conversation and also to see that this direction is maintained. Suppose the helper has as his goal to create a calm atmosphere. He will achieve this by asking the client, after a brief introduction, to say something about his problem while he, the helper, listens. The client is afraid to start, however, and becomes restless because of this imposed 'calm' atmosphere. Then the helper, though holding on to his goal, that is, promoting a calm atmosphere, will have to choose other means than merely listening. To choose another example: a client has trouble concentrating on his homework. As an outcome goal it was agreed that first the question would be considered whether his study methods were in need of improvement; this turns out not to be the case. While talking, the 'problems at home' are touched upon. The outcome goal is then shifted to a discussion of these problems and to finding ways to reduce them.

Thus, when things go well, it will gradually become clear during the helper's contact where the trouble lies with a client. The goals can then be formulated more clearly, and also the ways in which these goals can be attained, can be determined. However, it will often become apparent that the set goal has not been attained. What has gone wrong? Has the outcome goal not been sufficiently well defined? Is it unattainable or is something else wrong? Or, if the outcome goal is a good one, has the helper chosen the wrong process goals? Is he too passive or has he perhaps taken too much initiative?

It is important for the helper to be aware of process and outcome goals during the interview. One reason for this is that first, when the goals are kept clearly in mind, it is easier to evaluate where the helping situation needs adjustment if there is no progress in reaching the goal.

A second reason why it is worthwhile to set certain goals and to evaluate achievements against the goals set, concerns our preference for minimal intervention by the helper, as was already evident from the discussion of counselling philosophy and theory in Chapter 2. When a client needs no more than space and understanding to formulate, review, and solve his problem himself, the helper should do no more than offer space and understanding. When the client is not sufficiently helped by this and does not know how to deal with his problem, it is then the turn of the counsellor to offer new insights to help the client to look at his problem from a different angle. When that proves to be sufficient, then again the helper should do no more than offer insight. Finally, when this insight does not lead to action on the part of the client, then it is time for the helper to assist the client in such a way that he can learn to carry out the actions to achieve his goal.

It is clear from this brief discussion of minimal intervention that the helper should always be ready to step back as soon as the client is capable of solving problems himself. This means that the helper also has to decide with the client when that moment has come. This may occur at any point in the helping process. Obviously it is then useful to fix one more evaluation point – a follow-up interview – in order to review the decisions taken and see if they were right.

The roles of the helper

We have explained that the helper should adapt his strategy in a flexible way, depending on the goals that unfold during the counselling process. In order to show some congruity in this behaviour, the helper should adopt a certain role towards the client. This role may be altered as the interview progresses. In the next paragraphs we shall describe four roles of the helper.

The confidant

Someone approaches the helper with a personal problem and wants to talk about it to try to find a solution. What is the helper's response? Rogers says: bring calm and trust to the situation and create an atmosphere of security. This can be achieved by the helper accepting the client unconditionally and by being congruent and transparent himself. At the beginning, listening and empathic reactions are important. The client can then express his thoughts and emotions freely, while his being accepted by the counsellor leads to greater confidence. This is necessary; after all, people find it risky to share their problems with others. They thereby reveal themselves and make themselves vulnerable. For this reason the helper has to continue to accept the client and thus play the role of 'confidant'.

The counsellor, in his role of confidant and sounding-board, helps the client to talk through and thereby think through the issues that trouble him. When quietly considering and looking for words to talk about his impressions, memories, and emotions, the client is simultaneously differentiating, reorganizing, and integrating those thoughts and in new and better ways doing what we referred to earlier as 'information processing'. This also implies that he can introduce nuances and new insights into his thinking. This process of differentiation and integration (discussed in Chapter 3) is promoted by his thinking through and expressing himself. In Wexler's view trust in the helper also plays a considerable part, since the process of differentiation and integration of material on personal problems is a difficult one. People all have their own ways of processing information about themselves and their world in such a way as to keep an orderly and surveyable overall picture in their minds. New experiences and events often give rise to confusion, anxieties, and other emotions. Only when a new order has been attained will the client regain his calm. The understanding and calm on the part of the helper are supportive in spite of the client's restlessness. When the helper remains quiet and conveys reassurance when confronted with emotions and new ideas, when he shows his confidence that all will end well and does not immediately jump out of his chair to get glasses of water or handkerchiefs, or try to find immediate solutions to the problem in order to calm his client down, the latter will be able to tolerate uncertainties better and seek a new order himself, while being strengthened in his feeling of confidence.

The constructive insights engendered by the client himself may bring him closer to a solution to his problems. He sees more sides to the question (differentiation) and gets an overview (integration), but in a more balanced manner. The genuine acceptance expressed by the counsellor stimulates this process by giving him confidence to continue to take the initiative. That may be highly unusual for the client: the solution is not found by the expert, at least not for the moment. The helper who uses the cooperation model – remember also the example of Michael in Chapter 2 – makes optimal use of the client's capacity for solving his own problems.

When the client is reluctant to express his feelings, he will sometimes prefer to talk first about a less burdened subject. In this way he can test the helper more or less consciously: 'How is he reacting? Can he be trusted? Does he think I'm silly?' The helper's initial reactions are of vital importance. What kind of attitude does he communicate: quiet encouragement to continue? Or does he show signs of impatience: 'When will he get to the real problem?' Even slight reactions of the helper are highly significant for the client. To build up a trusting relationship – to truly become a confidant – is a delicate process, in which the client, very sensitive to reactions, is trying to probe the helper. Sometimes, however, a client can be quite blunt and provocative: 'Let's see how far we can go!'

There is yet another reason why the helper should adopt a receptive attitude at the beginning of the contact. Only by being accessible to anything the client says and by encouraging the client to put thoughts into words, can the helper form a picture of the experiential world of the client. This is important because, as we already indicated in Chapter 2, we wish to work from the frame of reference of the client. Moreover, we believe on the basis of Wexler's theory that this can hardly be done in any other way. After all, the client has his own way of putting things together (information processing system) which is very complicated. Where fundamentals are concerned, any changes in that system, as we said earlier, cause confusion and anxiety. This means that we should not force our way into this delicate structure with our own ideas of 'we know what is best for you'. This could lead to a refusal to accept this new information out of a sense of self-protection; in other words, of not really processing it. After all, the client has worked his whole life building his own picture of the world. Even if there are some faults in it, he will not easily let it be taken away from him. We have familiar expressions for this reaction: 'She doesn't want to accept this'; 'I can't get anywhere with this'; 'He finds that too much of a threat'. The gap between the client's existing view and the helper's proposed view may be too great. The helper may even be completely in the wrong with his proposed changes; that can also happen!

So far we have dealt with one general way that the helper, in his role as confidant, can influence the client. By general influence we mean the helper's attitude of interest shown in the client as a person, thus encouraging him to tell his story. The helper has a second, more specific, direction-giving influence which is related to the helper's responses to the actual specific things the client tells him. When the helper shows a particular interest in certain themes and topics that the client brings up, these will begin to stand out as important to the client, and be viewed with greater interest by him. As a consequence of the helper's reactions the client will be willing to say more on the subjects in which the helper has shown interest. In short, the helper has considerable influence on the client and on the interview even if his attitude is one of reserve in his role of confidant and sounding-board.

Is the role of confidant enough? Certainly the helper, by being a receptive and attentive listener, is to the client a relaxed and interested figure. But the helper may want to be more than an attentive listener. He will ask himself all sorts of questions about the experiental world of the client, but the answers may still elude him – for instance, when the latter continues to talk vaguely and incompletely about his problems and goals. This implies that the helper would like to share his views on the problem in order to check with the client whether these are right, acceptable, or worth considering. Thus we come to the second role of the helper.

The communicative detective

Frequently the role of confidant and sounding-board proves to be sufficient. The client, by talking calmly and unburdening himself, has put things in order, and by doing so has reached a better understanding of his situation and can carry on by himself. If so, stop helping!

But suppose that the client is not sufficiently helped by this. The discussion runs in circles, the client talks about all kinds of things, but remains vague. What then? Well, then the helper does more than just listen. He does something with the information that comes to him. There are good and not so good ways of doing this. He may, for example, categorize the information for himself and try to label the client in some of the following ways: 'full of uncertainty, lack of courage, fear of not performing well – aha! a typical inferiority complex'. While this superficial classification or a diagnosis may be useful as a rough description of the general impression and behaviour of the client, it is less suitable for doing something with it, let alone conveying to the client.

Detection applied to the client's subjective world

We have already shown that it is not the task of the helper to assess the problems of the client in this diagnostic way, that is, in terms that fit into the frame of reference of the helper. What the helper must do is to find out how the client thinks and feels about the significant events in his life. Only if he knows how the client himself functions, and construes his world, can he try to find solutions that will be accepted by the client, because they are in line with his ways of thinking. To characterize these activities of the helper we introduce the role of the 'detective'. In this role the helper has to ask several crucial questions: how does this client interpret events in his life? What is his way of thinking about his world and how is this view developed? These are important questions, for if the helper can get a clear insight into the client's experiencing process, it will be easier for him to detect the knots and twists in this process which are troubling the client. The helper who directs his attention towards the client with these questions in mind automatically becomes 'client-centred'. He is curious and will not quickly think, 'Oh, I see; oh, I have that too; so many people have that.' He will direct his attention to the individual characteristics of the client. In short, like a detective he will want to find out exactly how 'it' works. This makes work as a helper exciting: to be attentive to what can be found out about the client's own world by what he says, does, or shows in other ways. The helper is busy concentrating: he does not immediately want to offer a solution, nor does he ask himself, 'Am I sufficiently "congruent" or "genuine" and do I accept the client?' Concentration on and interest in the client's functioning are the central aims of the helper at this point and this goal makes him almost effortlessly congruent without any preoccupations of his own.

To be generally client-centred does not, however, tell the helper what he should concentrate on. As we have seen, Wexler shows that there are three important processes taking place when people interpret and process information: selection, differentiation, and integration. This classification may guide the helper in focusing his attention. First, the helper can ask himself: how and what does the client select to talk about? What does he omit? For example, the helper in Chapter 3 hears his client talk about his wife's negative qualities (see p. 35) and notes, 'no positive qualities – all negative'. Or he hears a housewife talk about her duties to the family and observes, 'no reference to her own rights'. He will also notice how some things mentioned during the conversation are used only partially or inconsistently by the client in the further course of the conversation. He tries to hold on to such items to try to form from them a picture of the way in which the client biases his selection of information.

A second question that the helper may ask is: how does the client differentiate and integrate? When these two are well-balanced they may result in experiential growth. When there is no progress or change in the client's problem, something is wrong. We now turn to this type of difficulty.

Too little differentiation and too quick integration The client is inclined to keep his world surveyable so he can picture it as a whole. New information is immediately slotted into an existing mental framework. When this is done too hastily, that is, when the client quickly jumps to conclusions, the capacity for distinguishing relative shades of meaning and subtle nuances is limited: 'All Scottish people are tight-fisted'; 'I am alone, and nothing can be done about it.' Inviolable certainties and absolutist, all-or-nothing thinking define his experience. Exceptional occurrences hardly ever result in more relative thinking or more differentiation. It appears that 'nothing ever happens', for the person does not let anything intrude into the world as he perceives it. One result may be that his outlook may become ever more rigid. The helper becomes aware of this process by the client's tendency to think and speak in clichés: 'The fact remains that. . . .' A consequence of this type of thinking includes feelings of listlessness, dullness, uselessness, and more severe emotional disturbances such as depression (Beck, Rush, Shaw, and Emery 1979). The client is incapable of actively shaping his world and thus undergoes little variety in his feelings. He may just be tired or sad and in that case he needs a certain amount of time to pull himself together. When, however, there is no reason for such an assumption, the 'detective' should hold on to this discovery and try to find out how the client thinks he is performing in other areas.

Too much differentiation and too little integration Another pattern is found in those clients who absorb too much information and differentiate this information too much, who see too many nuances and cannot make all this into a clearly defined whole. This inability to take a 'bird's eye view' may be caused either by the intrusion of sudden changes in the client's environment or by his own tendency to look for and see too many sides to a question. 'Everything is related to everything', according to these clients, and they can no longer distinguish a pattern. They let anything come into their heads and they sometimes talk about all kinds of things, skipping from one subject to another. This situation leads to uncertainty, confusion, and anxiety. In such an interview everything is poured out to the helper who may also think, 'Good heavens, let's keep calm, or I will lose the thread myself', while he may also become anxious: 'How can I keep things in hand?'

It is evident that when the process of differentiation and integration does not run smoothly, the helper must do something. To let a client wander about in a mist of vagueness will not help him at all, nor will the continued lending of a sympathetic ear to the stream of uncoordinated details. On the contrary, the client comes to realize still more how complex and badly organized his world is, and will become even more anxious.

Detection applied to the client's objective world

Before the helper as 'detective' can bring any changes into the experiential world of the client, he (the helper) should also consider the objective world that the client in reality faces. It is difficult to get a clear picture of the issues the client is involved in in his daily life. These are mainly – or even only – accessible through the eyes of the client. Thus the helper does not know the real facts and he needs those to find out how a client 'constructs' his own experiential world. Therefore the helper will have to try to get as close to the 'facts' as possible. Often the only way is to question the client. The helper who hears his client say, 'My wife does not love me any more' will ask, 'From what do you deduce that?' He will not be fobbed off with vague phrases about behaviour, feelings, and thoughts of the client and the people around him, for they do not help him much.

But even before the helper gets answers from the client to his fact-finding questions, these same questions may set the client thinking. They may make him consider matters he used to take for granted: 'Yes, how did I come to that conclusion?' the husband of the non-loving wife may think. Here again our advice is, when more specific questions prove to be stimulus enough to solve the client's problems, well and good: stop further explanations. This is not the time for the helper to give his exposé of the problem just to show how clever he is! Therefore our advice here is: stop counselling.

Communicating to the client

Up to now we have spoken in this section of the 'detective' but not yet about the 'communicative' aspect mentioned in the heading. The word 'detective' suggests a person keen to catch the perpetrator by collecting and combining facts in an inscrutable manner. He poses the questions while leaving the other person in the dark about the reason for these questions and the purpose they may serve.

In Chapter 2 we have stressed the importance of cooperation and clarity with regard to the client. This does not fit in with the picture of the detective who is vague about his methods, thoughts, and motives as a background for his actions.

By speaking of the *communicative* detective we want to emphasize that the helper should tell all he can about the issues under consideration – at least, in so far as it makes for improved communication with and stimulation for the client. This implies, for instance, that he explains to the client why he is asking these specific questions: 'In order to get a clear picture of the way in which you and your wife treat each other, I do not want to have only your opinion but also want to know what happens, what you both do, for example, when you are discussing a problem. Tell me . . .'

It may seem rather cumbersome to explain the background to all the questions one asks, though this explanation does not have to be very extensive or detailed. But it is useful for the helper to realize that the thoughts and considerations which are not put into words may make his questions and behaviour harder to understand. Moreover, by failing to express one's thoughts, a chance may be missed to teach the client something, namely, how the detective tries to gather and process information and why he thinks it worthwhile to go deeper into certain things. 'Thinking aloud', a skill which will be discussed in greater detail in Chapter 6, is an important cornerstone for satisfactory cooperation between helper and client.

In his role of detective the helper will mainly try to obtain a better picture of the client's experiential world. By his communicativeness he may set the client thinking in a new direction. Sometimes, however, that is not enough and he will have to explain to the client more emphatically and explicitly how there are other and better ways to look at and deal with his problem.

The teacher

The question arising after the detective has done his work is how the helper can convey his alternative views of the client's problem without putting the client's experiential world under strain and without damaging the cooperative alliance. We believe that this can be achieved by a smooth transition from the role of detective to that of teacher: not the authoritative teacher who always knows best, but one who tentatively lays other perspectives before the client, so that the latter can look at their significance for himself. The helper's role is more an explanatory one. He tries to explain to the client that problems can be considered in a different way, and to show how this may be done. Even if the 'facts' remain the same, one can look at them in another way, which is an important theme in this book.

Whether this conveying of a different viewpoint is also effective, is another matter. One problem is that we do not know beforehand to what extent a client can make changes in his experiential process. The helper has to ask himself to what extent the personality and capacities of the client form an obstacle to change. Furthermore, it is difficult to assess how all kinds of acquired ways of doing things and of thinking can be 'un-learned' or corrected. We know that in general people are able to learn and unlearn many things, certainly under secure conditions. That fact may be something for the helper to hold on to when he wants to help people with their problems.

In the second place the helper should take care that his own observations and interpretations of the client's thoughts and experiences are not affected by his own prejudices (rigid ways of information-processing by the helper himself). There is no real objectivity where one's experience of certain situations is concerned. Everybody constructs his own reality. And why should the reality as seen by the helper be better than that seen by the client? Nevertheless, the helper's contribution may be fruitful. Perhaps his views on the matter are less troubled by side issues and less distorted by the problems, while he also has more experience, supplemented or corrected by his knowledge of psychology. Perhaps, too, the fact that the helper openly chooses a different standpoint, literally or figuratively, is sufficient reason for a different viewpoint on the part of the client (James 1899). The chance that the helper achieves this will be greater when the client does not have to take too great a step to arrive at that point of view.

Now the concept of 'empathy' is once more at issue. The 'teacher' is the one who tries to put into words for the client the understanding which he acquired by his empathic attitude as 'confidant' and 'detective'. We have seen that Rogers considers it the task of the helper to clarify 'vaguely known meanings' of the client. Wexler also considers it the teacher's task to keep close to the experiential world of the client, though he allows the helper to introduce new perspectives. Thus a gradual transition is made from someone who merely shows his understanding for the client's situation to the teacher who introduces possible new perspectives for the client to consider, and which may work as an 'eye-opener'.

We have described the teacher as a helper who primarily assists the client in learning to think differently and come to a different perception. When this perception results in the client learning to accept his problems or in these problems being reduced or even disappearing altogether because of these new viewpoints, nothing more need be done. Frequently, however, these new insights require action, a different way of doing things. Which brings us to the next role of the helper.

The coach

Help is not effective when the client only demonstrates his new insights in conversation with the helper. The point is whether the client can do something with this new perspective on his problems in the reality of his daily existence. Only by bringing the newly acquired views into practice can they be tested for their true value. The helper's consulting room is no more than the 'hothouse' where the new ideas germinate. Hence it is also the duty of the helper to assist the client if necessary in the execution of his plans in his own environment.

We call this role of the helper the 'coach'. That concept brings to mind someone who in the background explains to the player or athlete the game or technique, who guides him during his training, encourages him to continue, and prepares him for achievement. But that achievement is realized by the player himself according to his own judgement and his own sense of responsibility. At most the coach is seated on the sideline and observes how things are going. Afterwards the coach takes care of the player, and successes and failures are reviewed and worked through. Later still, the results are discussed; together they correct mistakes and bring about improvements. The player prepares himself for a new attempt to perform to the best of his ability.

The same action pattern develops between helper and client. At the very moment that the client says rather hesitantly, 'Yes, I'll have to try it that way, but how do I go about it?' the helper becomes a coach. He helps to realize the insights which have been propagated or transferred by the teacher, after he has, as a detective and confidant, gathered the necessary material. This part of the helping process is far from easy, because the helper has to present a combination of restraint, in order not to force the client, and stimulation, to help the client across certain thresholds. Often the client will start to behave in a way not apparent before. To the helper this can mean two things. We call to mind Bandura's distinction, referred to in Chapter 4, between knowing what action is needed to get a certain result ('outcome expectations') and the conviction of the client that he can personally carry out those actions successfully ('efficacy expectations'). In the former case the client may have the knowledge of the required behaviours. In the latter case a client might say, 'I know I should do it like that, but I cannot.' In such a case the client is aware of how things should be done, but is afraid of doing them himself because of his low 'efficacy expectations'. This is where the coach comes in to train the client in the desired behaviour until his sense of 'self-efficacy' is high enough to try it himself.

We will not here go into the principles involved in the preparation of the client for a new approach. These will be discussed in Chapter 8. But it is relevant to remark that an adequate preparation of the client puts a considerable burden on the coach (helper). Perhaps it concerns actions of the client in an area which he has avoided up to now. In that case the planning must be aimed at maximizing the chance of success while possible failures are not taken too seriously. Otherwise there may be a danger of avoidance behaviour being reinforced: 'Even with all this help I have failed (again); perhaps I'd better stop altogether.' But client and helper should also be forewarned that, even when behaviour change is successful, it is very difficult to predict the effect of the proposed changes on the client's environment. There is a fair chance that when problematic behaviour is no longer 'problematic', it will lead to positive reactions from the environment. On the other hand, we have to bear in mind that the 'environment' has certain fixed ideas and expectations about the client as a person with his (special) behaviour. When this behaviour is changed, the balance between the client and those around him is disturbed. And then what happens? The changes in the interaction between the client and his environment may lead to new problems.

Even when the client has decided not to do anything tangible about his problem but to accept it, he may change noticeably in his behaviour. When a man has come to realize that he should stop getting annoyed by his boss, succeeds in doing so, and stops criticizing the boss at home, his wife may react with concern: 'What is the matter, you are so quiet, are you all right?' And that situation should also be dealt with successfully by the client. We do not want to suggest that helping with one problem always leads to another – the wife may also say, 'Hey, you've changed for the better' – but that we should be aware of the possibility of complications.

It is the coach's job to guide and help his client by discussing and evaluating the outcome of his experiments with his new behaviour in real life. What were the client's experiences? Did his new insight also 'work' in reality? Could the client do what he thought he could do? How did his environment react, etc.? The experiences gained by the experiments with new forms of behaviour in practice are a rich source of information for coach and client. From that they can assess whether the client has profited from the new behaviour.

The above discussion should make clear that it is not our intention to view the helper's roles as being strictly separate. They overlap and complement each other. The next role cannot be properly fulfilled without the previous one. The function of this description is mainly to give the helper something to hold on to, to judge for himself how he should choose his role in the light of developments in the client's problems and the way he deals with them.

To speak in terms of roles is not to suggest that this behaviour is superficial or unnatural. How each helper gives shape to these roles depends on his personal options, affinities, and preferences. Just as good acting requires that one identifies with various roles, so the helper should act in such a way that the question of real or unreal does not arise (see also p. 21).

In order to give the helper some further insight into the helping process, we will now discuss a helping model in three stages, in which the roles discussed above have a place.

A helping model

We will now outline a helping 'model' – a framework which contains a set of logical, practical guidelines for carrying out counselling, based on the principles discussed above. The function of this model is to place the various goals of counselling in a planned sequence so that the helper can keep an overall view and direction. We draw upon the model developed by Egan (1975, 1982), in which three principal stages are distinguished.

Problem clarification

In the first stage of an interview helper and client should get a better idea of the client's problems: clarification of the problem. Since personal matters are not easily shared with others, the beginning will often be hesitant and cautious. This is a necessary prelude. It is the helper's task to create some clarity about the course of events and invite the client to say what is bothering him. The helper listens; the client finds he can speak freely or, if he is still afraid to do so, that he is also permitted to evade the real issue for a little while longer.

Then, as soon as there is the beginning of good rapport, the helper will encourage the client to elaborate and to explore the problem. The client tries to put his problems into words and learns to trust the helper and his reactions. At this stage the aim is not to make choices, to indicate in detail what the problem is or what should be done about it. In other words, the helper is not yet engaged in setting outcome goals. When during the interview it appears, for instance, that the client has problems with his parents, the helper should not immediately jump in with questions about how the client thinks he can improve that relationship, what should be agreed upon as a goal and how to achieve that. The goal at this stage should be directed not to such an outcome, but simply to enabling the client to explore his thoughts, feelings, and actions related to the problem – a process goal.

The helper does not confine himself here to merely paying attention. He strives to keep a certain order in the discussion where necessary and to making vague statements more concrete. He also aims at enhancing cooperation with the client, and at promoting a joint search and clarification. Attention remains focused on the (experiential) world of the client. For himself the helper will attempt on the basis of that world to look for ways to get a perspective on the problems different from that of the client. We have in mind here the role of detective. However, he continues to be cautious and tentative in his interpretations and suggestions and he keeps sufficient space for more and different nuances in his view of the client. We deliberately say here 'view of the client' and not of the problem, because at this stage the helper should be careful not to direct his thinking exclusively to the problem. Perhaps more is involved here.

Summary

First stage: Problem clarification

> *Goal for the helper*: to achieve good rapport, to get a better idea of the problems both from the client's and from his own viewpoint.
> *Goal for the client:* to obtain a clearer and more precise picture with regard to his problems.
> *Task for the helper:* to inspire confidence and trust, to listen attentively, to clarify, to put some order in the discussion, and to develop ideas of his own without uttering them as yet.
> *Task for the client:* to try to express his problem, to examine it from all sides, to tell which facts, feelings, and actions are involved.

Gaining new insights

In the discussion with the client the helper cannot keep on exploring indefinitely. At any rate the helper whose aim it is to assist the client in doing something about his problem, should be wary of exploration leading simply to more and more issues being involved in the problem. That can soon lead to the situation where client and helper cannot see the wood for the trees.

There is a misconception that by a continuing analysis and exploration one gets closer to the 'root' of the problem. This is a dangerous assumption where the solving of personal problems is concerned. From Bandura's basic formula $\left(\begin{smallmatrix} & P & \\ B & \longleftrightarrow & E \end{smallmatrix}\right)$ can be concluded how complicated human functioning really is. The longer we talk about a problem and the more we bring in side issues, the more complicated things get. We do not find a clear 'root', but a muddle of possible causes. This very fact is often the cause of obsessive 'brooding'. The more intelligent and creative people are in looking for possible causes, the more they will find such causes, so that in the end they become increasingly entangled in the problem; they can no longer find a way out.

It is clear that the process of exploration involves a considerable degree of what Wexler calls differentiation – analysing a problem into many separate parts – and that there are considerable dangers in doing this and only this. As the picture grows more complex, it is essential to integrate the parts as well. The two processes of differentiation and integration should go hand in hand. The quantity and diversity of information should not, however, go beyond the integration abilities of helper and client.

The goal of the second stage then is to help the client get a more precise and better defined view of his problem – a better differentiation and integration. Here the helper starts to play the part of the teacher helping his client to put his thoughts in a new order. It is tempting to speak here in terms of a 'deepening' of insight or of 'true' causes being indicated. In our opinion these words suggest faulty ideas. The key word is not 'true' or 'deep' but 'different'. By using the word 'different' we also avoid giving a value judgement. 'Different' is more neutral than 'true' or 'deep'. And this neutrality is necessary because the helper does not yet know if 'different' will also prove to be 'better'. Therefore a change must be made in the client's way of seeing things to find a way out of the maze.

The helper will make use of ideas which have already originated in the first stage and which will be further developed in the second. He will present to the client his views of the elements of the problem. The teacher is at work again. He looks for 'knots' in the client's thinking, drawing on the theories discussed in Chapters 3 and 4. How does the client think, feel, and do, and what are the salient points in his way of thinking, experiencing, and acting? The helper will also try to assist the client in finding the main thread in a series of seemingly unconnected facts and problems.

This necessarily means that the helper also contributes to the selection and restriction of themes under discussion. Selecting a problem or partial problem for further discussion is a difficult step. Neither the helper nor the client may know whether the subject selected is indeed the most relevant part of the problem. Nevertheless it is necessary for an orderly working method to keep on making choices, while it is essential to the cooperating process that the client is fully involved in the making of these choices. It helps to clarify the issues and enhances the sharing of responsibility. The selection of themes becomes less of a burden once the helper and his client realize that they can always turn back if they really get lost in the maze of personal complexities. This will become evident when the (sub)goal is not reached as a result of the choices made. Once again the importance of clear goals is demonstrated. Only with such goals in mind can certain activities be adjusted where necessary.

This stage demands a greater resilience of the client. It is quite possible that the information the helper gives him about himself is difficult to accept and digest. His characteristic way of thinking and doing – which up to now had been best for him – is affected. This may hurt (at first) because some of the things he holds dear are shown to be questionable. There may be (temporary) insecurity and confusion in the client, because the old familiar way of dealing with information is altered. At this stage the main goal is: to help in gaining insight into the problem to such an extent that a solution or several solutions are within reach.

Summary

Second stage: Gaining new insights

  Goal for the helper: to achieve a more differentiated yet integrated view of the problem both for the client and for himself; selecting problems for discussion.

  Goal for the client: to obtain a clearer, more differentiated, yet integrated picture of the problems; insight; choice of problems.

  Task for the helper: to listen attentively, to clarify, and bring order into the problem; to give the client an idea of the connecting links by giving an alternative view.

  Task for the client: to strive to put his problems into words, to explore, to strive to consider and digest the helper's opinions.

Treatment of the problem

The title of this third stage is partly misleading, because from it might be concluded that treatment is not dealt with in the previous stages. Seeking clarification and insight are also 'treating' activities, but they remain confined to the thinking level: to discussing possibilities and consequences. Now we come to the stage in the discussion where the client seeks answers to such questions as: 'Yes, I now understand what caused the problem, but what can I do about it?' The goal of the third stage is therefore to *do* something about the problem.

The question is how to give shape to this 'doing'. We believe that the client himself should decide which problem(s) he wants to tackle first. The responsibility for that choice lies with him; it is his life. It is also up to the client to select ways and means to achieve that chosen purpose. Here the helper can make important contributions, for it is obvious that the client does not know how to do this alone. Even when the means to this end are known and the client believes that he will succeed in putting his plans into practice, it is still not easy for him to go into action. However tempting it is for the helper to encourage him forcefully, enforced pressure can cause considerable damage. At this stage, too, the client needs to be accepted with his courage but also with his fear of the unknown, which may even result in his being frightened off the intended action. The client should have the freedom (after due consideration) not to act at all, even if the helper regrets this.

After choices about the goals and means of achieving them have been made, the next step for client and helper is to decide together as clearly and concretely as possible how the desired goal can be reached and what sort of (new) behaviour is needed for this. However, for the helper it is not enough to instruct the client how best to promote and facilitate new behaviour. In his role as coach, which becomes important at this stage, the helper must also find out how the client's new behaviour works out in practice. What does the client deduce from this new experience?

Summary

Third stage: Treatment of the problem

> *Goal for the helper:* definition of the goals aimed at, choice of instruction and action programmes, promoting an effective course of action.

Goal for the client: definition and choice of goals and achieving these goals.

Task for the helper: to list all the options; to encourage and promote choices; to draw up action programmes; to support the client in carrying out these programmes.

Task for the client: to choose what problems to tackle and to what purpose; to (dare to) carry out action programmes; to report his experiences.

The model in practice

The description of the helping model may give the impression that in practice it is easy for a helper to conduct counselling very much in accordance with the model. If only this were true! Often it is very difficult to keep some order in the discussion and even more difficult to carry out certain plans. Even so, a model, including goals and means, is important in order to determine how the helper is to work, to look at the actual course of events, and to find out the reasons for any deviations from the plan. The client can also participate in this search and thus assist in finding a solution. Moreover, the model enables the helper to consider after a counselling session how things really stand: how did the interview go, at what stage did problems occur, did I pick the right role, how far did we digress, what shall we discuss next on the basis of all this? We will now comment on the use of the model in practice.

Cumulative building of goals and tasks

The three-stage model described above gives the helper a tool for organizing a course of counselling with a client. It should not be concluded from this that there are clearly marked transitions at which helper and client suddenly change their goals and tasks. The transitions are often very blurred, particularly between the first and second stage. More importantly, however, the helper does not completely stop doing one thing and start doing something entirely different. There is a cumulative building of goals and tasks. At stage two attention and exploration remain just as important, but to these are added some new elements. Every new interpretation introduced by the helper requires further exploration into the client's reactions. The client, too, will have to consider whether he can identify these new elements. In the third stage, when action is undertaken, the previous stages remain especially important for an adequate discussion of the client's new experiences.

Applying the stages to problems

When using a model we should realize that the stages do not apply to the interview as a whole but rather to each problem as it emerges. Suppose we are talking with a client about his study problems and are making some progress. We are already at stage two when the client realizes that his tendency to postpone working may have something to do with his fear of discovering that he is not really bright enough for this particular topic of study. As long as he does not really apply himself, he can always blame his poor marks on his laziness: 'Once I really start working, I will do better.' In the course of the discussion it emerges that his parents may have something to do with this; apparently their attitude is one of: 'In our family there is no such thing as being not bright enough.' The helper responds by suggesting a discussion about the relation between the client and his parents. And for that discussion stage one (clarification of the problem) is started once more.

In short, as we said before, in a person-oriented approach of the client we sometimes come to a separate and sometimes to a combined discussion of the different themes and problems at different stages. In a situation with more than one problem the model helps to make things more surveyable to both client and helper.

The model is not all-powerful

The ultimate goal of discussing and dealing with problems is to remedy certain difficulties. We have seen how the model can have a role in this. However, the behaviour of people, helpers and clients alike, is far too complex and unpredictable to be able to say that the model should always be adhered to. There are situations in which stages of the model are either drastically shortened or even skipped altogether. This may be caused by the client, the nature of the problem, or the helper's preference.

A client who has difficulty in discussing his problems has little use for lengthy and fruitless attempts by the helper to bring about a meaningful discussion. Thus the helper should not rigidly insist that first stage one and two have to be gone through before it is the turn of stage three! Rather, he should take more initiative at the beginning than he would with a fluent talker. He will try to relate to the world the client lives in. This will frequently mean that there will be less talk about the problems and possible solutions. The helper will get his information by asking specific questions and then try to help the client to learn other behaviour patterns.

It may be useful with clients who have already talked at length about 'their problem' not to take too long to explore and introduce new insights. Instead, the helper can encourage the client to do something about the problem which has already been so carefully analysed, and thus find out where the obstacles for action are.

The nature of the problem may be another reason to use the model in a somewhat adapted form. A client enters hurriedly and announces that her husband is planning to leave home the next day and take the children with him. Clearly not the right moment to adopt an indulgent attitude such as: 'Please sit down, Mrs Smith. We will have a number of counselling sessions to see how we can deal with your problem.' Action is called for and that at very short notice. But even then, the helper should take the time to get acquainted, to create an atmosphere of calm and trust and try to get a clear picture of the problems before he can help.

In summary, we do not pretend that the model provides an applicable method in all situations. Crisis intervention demands a special approach. And there are many more situations in which the model should not be seen as an end in itself; it is a means. What we want to stress is the importance of checking whether deviations from the model are necessary for practical reasons.

Time is limited

With the desperate client described above we have introduced the factor of time. Often, though, it is not only the client who is pressed for time; the same goes for the helper, sometimes because he has other clients waiting, sometimes because other work is waiting.

It is clear that hastiness can be an obstructing factor in dealing with personal problems. We have repeatedly stressed the need for calmly exploring, introducing new insights, encouraging action, and again reviewing new obstacles in the execution of plans.

Haste may lead to the helper, not only undermining these goals, but also neglecting to pay attention to essential problems in his counselling, resulting in reduced effectiveness. He may then be forced to conclude that his efforts are wasted. We bring to mind the investigation by Lewin referred to earlier on the effect of different ways of giving advice and information. The most 'efficient' way to give information on how to behave in certain situations is in large groups of people in a traditional teaching situation. The effect of this, however, is limited. Also in certain counselling situations it is tempting, when pressed for time, to ask the client a great number of questions in order to get an idea of his problem quickly, and then give advice or prescribe a solution. This 'diagnosis–prescription' method, however, has many disadvantages. The fact that one is not personally involved with the client who in turn does not understand the whys and wherefores of the advice given, leads to his being disinclined, particularly with personal problems, to act upon this advice.

If the helper wants to achieve some result in spite of the lack of time, he will have to make an effort to pay attention to each of the stages of the model. Indeed, in such a hurried situation consultation with the client and clarity about the strategy is especially important.

On the other hand, when problems are being explored one is tempted just to go on and on for too long. Anyone may think of further problems or at any rate find more unpleasant aspects of his existence, and certainly the habitual worrier does this. It is not good for the client when the helper encourages all this worrying and soul-searching by continuing to pay attention to it. A timely formulation of goals can put a stop to this 'exploring'. And this 'timely' intervention is helped, naturally, when there is indeed little time – a constructive use of time pressure. Also, the introduction of insights and treatment can be helped to proceed more quickly. Research has shown that the effect of short-term help need not be any less than that of lengthy treatment (Butcher and Koss 1978). One significant factor is that some pressure of time motivates the client to be open about problems sooner and to work harder to get finished in time.

These considerations mean that the helper should clarify with the client not only the goals they are jointly aiming to reach and the methods to be used, but also the length of time agreed upon to reach this goal.

The goals, method, and time may all turn out to be different from those agreed at the beginning, but that is no argument against making such agreements on them beforehand. On the contrary, when the situation as regards end, means, and time is clear, unexpected developments and delays will sooner lead to questioning: 'What is the reason for this; has the problem been sufficiently analysed; has the proper goal been set; have means and available time been well chosen?' This offers an opportunity to make adjustments when necessary. An important question that the helper should ask himself at this point is: 'Do I have the right expertise to assist in the problems of this particular client?'

Without a deadline, voluntary or not, the counselling may drag on for a long time. For a helper who has at his disposal only a limited number of ways of helping – and who among us does not – it is of vital importance to recognize the point where there is too little progress in or even a worsening of the problem. We should then discuss this with the client and act accordingly. In this profession the courage to refer someone to others or even to end a contact is often proof of more expertise and sense of reality than to go on (sometimes for years) without any noticeable results.

The helper as a person

A question often asked by helpers in training is, 'What should one be like as a human being, as a personality, to be capable of helping others?' This question often arises from doubts about one's suitability as a person to help others: 'Am I suitable as a person to play the role(s) as a helper in an acceptable manner?'

There is no simple answer to this question, not in general terms and rarely in any particular case. Nevertheless, we need to pursue this question here – not by giving clearcut answers but by looking at several aspects of the problem, which may encourage the reader to look more closely at the prerequisites of the helper as a person.

A good human being?

As we discussed before in Chapter 3, Rogers pays considerable attention to the personal qualities a helper should possess to make the contact with the client into a fruitful relationship. Qualities such as acceptance, congruence, and empathy already indicate that the helper should be a broadminded, well-balanced, and sensitive person. However, anyone adhering strictly to these standards will quickly write himself off as a suitable helper. Rogers, however, is less strict, also with regard to himself. In a chapter on the building up of a helping relationship he lists ten questions (Rogers 1961). For example:

> Can I *be* in some way which will be perceived by the other person as trustworthy, as dependable, or consistent in some deep sense? (p. 50)

> Can I permit him to be what he is – honest or deceitful, infantile or adult, despairing or over-confident? (p. 53)

The plans expressed by these questions are fairly ambitious. Rogers therefore goes on to say:

> If I could, in myself, answer all the questions I have raised in the affirmative, then I believe that any relationships in which I was involved would be helping relationships, would involve growth. But I cannot give a positive answer to most of these questions. I can only work in the direction of the positive answer.
>
> (Rogers 1961: 56)

In the final sentence of this quotation we find an element that is expressed in Rogers' work quite often, namely the willingness to work towards becoming a better helper. This implies a willingness to learn. And this is possible only if the helper is prepared to be open to improvement through an attitude of self-criticism, or even more difficult, of taking the criticism of others to heart. Doubts about one's suitability as a helper and a willingness to work hard to improve this show a realistic view of the complex processes involved in helping people.

Up to now in this section we have mainly discussed the general attitude towards the client. However, a recurring theme in the humanistic-psychological literature is the functioning of the helper as an individual in daily life. Followers of Rogers (Carkhuff and Berenson 1967) generalize the optimal relationship between helper and client with a daily lifestyle: 'counseling as a way of life'. They expect from the 'good' helper, a 'whole' person, that he should be capable of functioning better than the client in all areas. He should be 'more advanced' in his development, should live 'more effectively' than the client. Egan (1982) even carries this idea so far as to paint a portrait of a helper which is an accumulation of good qualities ('He shows respect for his body through proper exercise and diet') without any qualification. Thus we get a picture of a person who is extremely successful, able to handle any problem, helpful, sociable, tidy, and always active, in short, someone who is quite unreal and, by ordinary human standards, not at all credible. In fact, the picture portrayed is rather like the Mr or Mrs Success figure featured in many advertisements in the media!

We may be exaggerating a little, but not much. We criticize this view because the idea of the 'good helper' contains the seeds of something that the really good helper should be very wary of, namely, the belief that he can set the right norms and criteria for good living for others. Egan, for instance, says that the helper should by his behaviour be a model, an example for the client. Admittedly, we know from social learning theory that (important) persons influence the behaviour of others. When, however, the helper wants to encourage the client to choose his own way to find solutions and new lifestyles, he should not show his own (counselling) behaviour too obtrusively as an example.

Rogers recognizes the danger of too much emphasis on the good qualities of the helper in general when he states, after discussing the necessary conditions for a good relationship:

> It is not necessary (nor is it possible) that the therapist be a paragon who exhibits this degree of integration, of wholeness, in every aspect of his life. It is sufficient that he is accurately himself in this hour of this relationship that in this basic sense he is what he actually is, in this moment of time.
>
> (Rogers 1957: 97)

We see from this quotation that the helper's behaviour should be optimal mainly in his relation with the client. By this Rogers implies that these need not be general characteristics, but only certain attitudes in a certain situation. We find this opinion insufficiently expressed by the authors mentioned above, such as Carkhuff and Berenson, and Egan. The helper need not pretend to be a better human being in all respects in order to be able to help a client. We are reminded of a well-known psychologist who in his daily life was often a shy, sometimes rude, and carelessly dressed person, entangled in many problems of his own. But in his contact with clients he was extremely wise, attentive, involved, and concentrating on searching for the right solution of their problems.

Must we conclude from what we have said that the state of mind of the counsellor is unimportant for good counselling, that his circumstances are unimportant? No, of course not. They are important when preoccupation with his own problems and concerns prevents him from dealing with the client in the way described in the previous chapters. The criterion for responsible helping is not whether the helper is capable of functioning 'well' according to middle-class standards in daily life. The criterion is whether he can dissociate himself sufficiently from his own lifestyle, his own opinions and problems, and put himself in the client's experiential world and concentrate on that. And that is a very difficult thing to do! Thus in the codes of practice for clinical psychologists in many countries the client's interests and the psychologist's competence are strongly emphasized, though one may look in vain for a maximum permissible body weight for psychologists!

A suspicious person?

If there is one cliché whose truth is demonstrated time and again on the basis of psychological research, it is that people are complex creatures. Just when we think we are sure we know something about somebody, then quite often even that knowledge is found to have many holes in it. This means that the helper is always in the precarious situation of having to be very careful of expressing certainties about his client as well as about himself, let alone the interactions between them. For these reasons some psychologists are very sceptical about the possibilities of professional help with personal problems, certainly on a scientific basis. Duijker (1978, 1980) has described and analysed this dilemma in which science demands factual proof and objectivity, but professional counselling seems in many ways to be a 'common sense', intuitive enterprise. Counselling goals can only ever be partially supported by science. However, we advocate that the effective helper should be familiar with, and use, a knowledge of the science of human psychology, and in particular should use such knowledge to give him objective insights that correct the subjective distortions his 'common sense' may give him. However, this is no easy task. For example, he must not see his own norms and standards as self-evident, and he must have the courage to look upon his own knowledge and methods as incomplete. These demands are high because it is difficult for people – including helpers – to be objectively aware of the standards by which they live and the methods and knowledge they use. To quote Duijker, speaking about psychologists:

> The mere fact that one studies or has studied psychology is no guarantee that one can see through one's own subjective standards, prejudices, shortcomings and childish desires. The helper's theoretical knowledge is no safeguard against the general human tendency to self-deception. To put it bluntly: the psychologist should learn to distrust not other people but himself first of all. And he certainly should not implicitly show himself as an example to others, even though this is a very human tendency. A psychologist should be critical, primarily of himself.
>
> (translation of Duijker 1978: 509)

Although he talks here about psychologists, the remarks apply to all helpers. But the question remains: are these shortcomings really so bad? Have trained helpers not learned to avoid certain mistakes in their contact with clients? We hope so, but there are indications that professional helpers should not be too smug.

In an extensive review about this subject Wills (1978) reports some remarkable results. Like ordinary people helpers have both positive and negative feelings towards their clients, depending on a number of factors such as the willingness or otherwise of clients to collaborate in the proposed treatment. Furthermore, helpers are inclined *more* than other people to see clients as 'maladjusted' and to stress the negative aspects of those clients. Helpers also tend to jump to conclusions about the personality of their clients on the basis of very little evidence. The reader may object, 'Yes, but helpers are probably right more often than other people.' This, however, is not the case. Wills' review shows that working in the therapeutic settings may lead to a loss of an unprejudiced view of clients and their problems. This 'professional distortion' requires correction by means of an attitude of 'distrust' expressed earlier in the quotation from Duijker. The 'distrust' advocated there is not the cynical distrust of the disillusioned helper who no longer believes in people and in help. It is a quality of wariness that leads to watchfulness, and which keeps one alert.

It is in the above sense that the reader should also interpret our critical appraisal of the helper. We do not intend to trip up the professional helper by pointing out all the things that can go wrong. Rather, we want to alert the helper, as part of the process of training, to the pitfalls involved in this work. By being aware of the pitfalls, the helper is better able to learn and make corrections when necessary. Being alert in this way is one of the justifications for professional help which adds to what is already being done spontaneously by lay helpers.

Self-protection

In many books on helping the reader is swamped with the rules, instructions, obligations, and responsibilities the helper should fulfil in the client's interest. This occurs also in this book. Poor helper! Teachers make their own demands and clients in need also expect a lot from him. Thus he is caught between the devil and the deep blue sea. In practice this often results in the helper believing that regretfully he can no longer cope with his work. There is every reason, therefore, to include in the heading 'what kind of person should the helper be?' some less romanticized and idealized elements as well.

The first principle we would suggest to helpers in training is to work in such a way that they remain sane themselves. That sounds selfish, but in the long run it is also beneficial for the client. What does that mean for the helper as a person? In the first place, it implies that the helper should be able to keep a certain distance from his clients and their problems. In order to keep that distance the helper has to realize that professional help is different from help given to friends, relations, and others close to him. It is useful in connection with this to list a few points of difference.

In the first place, the relation between helper and client is *asymmetrical*. Though the client relates his problems and due attention is paid to them, the helper is not supposed to do the same. Thus there is no question of the reciprocity so characteristic of a relation between friends.

The second point is: *whereas you try to keep a friend, a client is someone you try to lose*. The relation is a working relationship intended to reduce problems. When that objective has been reached, the relationship ends. Professional help is also usually confined to certain hours, determined by the helper. The 'balance' between helper and client is achieved by financial reward of the former. Whether this money is paid directly by the client or comes from a health service salary or other source is not at issue: the helper earns his living by helping, whether we are open about it or not.

Thirdly, the relation between helper and client is characterized by a certain *anonymity*. Ideally helper and client should have no other contact, business or personal, outside the helping sessions. This has a protecting as well as a liberating effect on both partners. The client can express himself freely and does not have to take the helper's feelings into account. The latter in turn should not become totally engrossed in his client's problems. His sympathy should not go so far that he can no longer control himself or the situation. The client has entrusted himself to him with the comforting thought that the helper will keep a clear head. This does not mean that the helper has cut-and-dried solutions, but that he keeps his distance. Standing 'above' the problem means that he does not easily panic and is in a better position to see a way out.

But does this distancing not work in the opposite direction to the involvement and empathy so necessary for a good helping relationship? Here we find ourselves in the area of one of those mysterious human characteristics: the capacity to work both with involvement and at a distance. The involvement is demonstrated by the concentration, the attending behaviour, the attempts to identify with the other's experiential world, the understanding shown, and the emotions evoked by this. The distance is shown by the control of the situation, the capacity to see what client and helper are doing together and separately, and to consider in the meantime what steps to take next, to control spontaneity. Distance should not be confused with coldness. It is controlled involvement, essential to give the client the impression and the certainty that the helper will remain supportive. Keeping a certain distance from the problem is especially useful because it forms the basis of some relativization of the problem and may even enable one to see (or show) its humorous side. Humour means a liberation from depressing seriousness. When a problem can be laughed about, much has been gained. For that to be possible, however, the helper must first let go of the deadly seriousness of helping. There is a special reason why we mention the aspect of humour in connection with the self-protection of the helper. For example, probably nowhere are blacker jokes made about human suffering than in field hospitals. It is an aid to survival in the midst of so much misery. Helpers who encounter great human misery must be allowed to joke about it sometimes among colleagues, or the burden becomes unbearable. This is not to make fun of patients but to relieve the tension.

An important characteristic of the helper which assists him in keeping that distance and capacity of relativization is that he should not have very high expectations of what he can do or change himself in order to offer help, nor of what the client must be able to see, do, or change to make this possible. The helper, too, can become the victim of excessively high standards and of the tension caused when these standards are not lived up to. We refer the reader to what was said in Chapter 4, about the tyranny of the ideal-image. Counselling can often help only a little, and furthermore the helper must exercise a lot of patience, but sometimes even a little help goes a long way.

In order to aid the helper in the use of the helping model and the various roles to be played, in the next three chapters we will deal with the skills and methods in a more concrete form.

Part two

Skills and strategies for helping

Chapter six

Problem clarification

Introduction

What skills should a helper have in order to put into practice the principles of good counselling discussed earlier? The concept of skill used here includes not only the traditional meaning of a sequence of learnt behaviours designed to achieve a goal effectively, but also the idea of a 'disposition' (De Groot 1975). 'Disposition' is derived from the Latin *disponere*, 'to set ready'. The concept is also found in the expression 'to be disposed to do something', meaning, 'to be willing to do something, to be available'. From this expression we see that it is a question of voluntariness here: a behavioural disposition is a behaviour that is 'at someone's disposal'; it can be made use of if desired. The professional helper needs a sufficient range of skills to be able to choose a combination that is most appropriate. This invariably means that trainee counsellors will be more effective if they learn new skills, to build on those they already have. This may sound technical, and it is. Every profession needs a sound technical basis and counselling is a profession in which the helper is his own instrument. It is therefore necessary consciously to learn these skills. With sufficient practice, this 'comes naturally'. The more skills and different behaviours one has acquired, the more one is at liberty to choose the behaviour to fit the particular situation. Thus we are not suggesting that a person should radically change in order to become a helper. What we are advocating is the skill-oriented approach which enables every helper to do what he himself thinks desirable by choosing from a series of skills.

Before discussing these skills further it is useful to make a distinction between the various kinds of training goal. We can differentiate between very general, abstract goals and very specific, concrete goals, as well as those in between. In counselling we have all kinds. First, at the most general level, we have such intention goals as being able to practise as a psychologist. In the second place there is a class of roughly defined goals, such as the ability to conduct a counselling interview. It is at this level that we also speak of 'interviewing models'. These goals can then be further distinguished into specific or operational goals, such as the ability to summarize relevant information from an interview. The operational goals can be indicated by the term 'interviewing techniques'.

A second distinction that we wish to make here is between mental skills – thinking strategies, if you like – and the actual counselling skills. An example of the former is to have at one's disposal a rough plan for a first interview. An example of the latter is being able to reflect a feeling. These categories are not mutually exclusive: the 're-flecting' of someone's feelings is always preceded by a mental operation.

The construction of the following chapters runs parallel with the stages of the Egan model discussed in Chapter 5: (1) problem clarification (this chapter); (2) gaining new insights (Chapter 7); and (3) strategies for treatment (Chapter 8).

Each stage has its own strategies and skills, which, however, need not necessarily be limited to these stages. Egan (1975) calls his model a 'developmental' model. This means that strategies and skills from preceding stages can also be incorporated in subsequent stages: 'The model is called developmental because it is composed of progressive interdependent stages' (Egan 1975: 28).

In this chapter we will be dealing with the first stage – problem clarification. We will discuss a number of *basic skills* which are needed to achieve this goal. Our choice of basic skills is mainly based on Ivey (1971).

The general strategy of a helper in the problem clarification stage is aimed at getting (together with the client) an idea of the problems: what they are, how the client sees them, how and when they have arisen, how serious they are, and their role in the whole of the client's life situation. Besides this it is also important to gather further data: age, job, social and economic status of the client, his functioning in his family, in school, work, and in his free time.

It is worth noting that the basic skills we will be describing are necessary not only during the various stages of a counselling interview, but also in other types of interview, such as a scientific interview, advice-giving, or breaking bad news: 'all interviewers, counselors, therapists should learn to listen, to attend to feelings and to interpret their clients' statements' (Ivey 1971: 6).

Goals of the initial interview

The *first goal* of the initial interview is to *establish a working relationship* with the client which enables him to feel safe enough to express himself. For a client who is not sure what is in store for him, such a first interview can appear rather awesome. There is an atmosphere of tension around 'mental' problems and most people regard talking about them with some anxiety. After all, you are in a very vulnerable position when you start to talk about your problems. Moreover, making a request for help is often seen as a sign of weakness; hence it is of primary importance to try to put the client at ease.

The *second goal* is to quietly *explore* the problems, without making the client feel that all sorts of things are expected of him. To facilitate this process, the helper should be able to listen carefully and show some understanding. As a result both the client and helper begin to get some insight into the client's problems and the world as he experiences it.

A *third goal* is to bring a sense of *order* to the problems. This is particularly important with a confused client.

Finally, a *fourth goal* is to make it as clear as possible what the client can expect from counselling. The client should be fully informed from the start. This also makes the first goal of creating an atmosphere of calm and safety easier to attain.

Basic attitude and basic skills

In order to do good counselling, the helper needs to have the right kind of client-centred attitude, discussed in Chapters 2, 3, and 5.

However, skills are needed to implement such an attitude in practice. However good his attitude is, if the helper cannot demonstrate this in his actual behaviour, the client will never notice it, no matter how praiseworthy! We have found that there is a considerable difference between possessing a good basic attitude and converting it into actions. Many students who endorsed the right attitude – of the client having responsibility and potential for finding solutions himself – nevertheless tended to come up with solutions within a very short time. This kind of error has been widely observed (Matarazzo, Philips, Wiens, and Saslow 1965). In short, good intentions do not guarantee professional skill.

What exactly are the skills we are talking about? In order to answer that question we will first give a survey of the basic skills necessary to achieve the goals mentioned above. These basic skills can be divided into two main categories, namely:

1. Listening skills
2. Regulating skills

By making use of his listening skills the helper gives the client an opportunity and encouragement to tell his story: the initiative is handed to the client.

The regulating skills are required to ensure that meaningful progress is made; meaningful, that is, in view of the purpose of counselling.

We give an overview below of the two sets of skills, and describe them in detail in the following sections.

Overview of basic skills[1]

Listening skills
'Non'-selective listening skills, attending behaviour:
  non-verbal behaviour
  verbal following
  silences
Selective listening skills:
  asking questions
  paraphrasing of content
  reflection of feeling
  concreteness
  summarizing
Regulating skills
  starting the interview
  making an initial contract
  goal-setting and goal-evaluation
  situation clarification
  thinking aloud
  ending the counselling interview

---

[1] These basic skills are demonstrated on a training videotape, Introductory Counselling Skills (see Appendix).

'Non'-selective means that the helper exerts little influence. He gives the client ample opportunity to tell his story and only responds by being attentive. These skills are intended to encourage and stimulate the client.

Selective skills mean those used by the helper to select certain aspects of the client's story which he thinks are important. The distinction we have made here should not be taken too literally, however, since 'non'-selection is virtually impossible. Even when the helper only listens attentively and encouragingly, he will – though he may not be aware of this himself – by his attitude and way of looking be more attentive to certain parts of the client's story than to others. That is why we have put the prefix 'non' between inverted commas. The same applies to the concept of 'non-directiveness' (see p. 30). We hope we have made it clear that we are referring to less directiveness in non-selective skills, and greater directiveness in selective skills.

Starting the interview and making an initial contract

Starting the interview and making an initial contract are the first things that the helper does, and they are both regulating skills. In the first place the helper will have to make some things clear right at the beginning. He himself takes the initiative here. A new client will not usually know exactly what to expect – how things are done in counselling – and the helper should therefore brief him as early as possible. A routine part of this briefing is that expectations on both sides are discussed. The best moment to do this depends, among other things, on the state of mind of the client. When, for instance, he is greatly confused ('in crisis'), a helper will not start with this but will first respond to this 'crisis' situation. When, however, a client after long hesitation but in a fairly quiet state of mind comes to a helper, perhaps even with an attitude of 'let's see what he has to offer me', the helper is advised to inform the client straightaway about his way of working, and then see if the client agrees with that, or whether he has other expectations. The helper can then consider these expectations and see if they are realistic and if they fit in with his way of working.

What should the helper include in his briefing? One part of it will certainly be the helper's own views on counselling, which in our case means emphasizing that it is a *joint undertaking with joint respon-*

sibility (see Chapter 2). The helper should also give a brief exposition of the general outline of counselling. Egan (1975) has the following to say on this:

> How much should the client know about the counseling model being used? As much as possible, I believe . . . . Counselors are often reluctant to let the client know what the process is all about. Some counselors seem to 'fly by the seat of their pants', and they cannot tell the patient what it's all about simply because they don't know what it's all about.
>
> (Egan 1975: 50)

In this book the emphasis lies on the helper being aware of what he does and to what *purpose* he does it. The essence of Egan's comment is that there is no need for the helper to keep such intentions to himself but that he should share them with his client. In fact Egan's three-stage model can be easily explained. Here is an example, in which we take up the dialogue with Michael's psychologist from Chapter 2:

> OK, Michael, you have come to talk about some concerns you have and we have three quarters of an hour for our session [clarity regarding the length of time!]. But before you begin I would like to tell you briefly about my usual method of working. I would first like us to be clear about what we are trying to do, and to get some idea about what is troubling you [Stage 1: Problem clarification]. That is what this first session is meant for, and we might need further sessions. Once we have a better idea of your concerns, we may decide to go deeper into them [Stage 2: Gaining new insights into the problem]. Finally we can consider what we can also *do* about them [Stage 3: Treatment of the problem]. What do you think, shall we try this? [Invitation to ask questions about the proposed three-stage process].

If the client agrees to the proposals, a basis for cooperation has been laid and both client and helper have the same frame of reference regarding the forthcoming tasks. If the client does not agree, they can discuss how the client would prefer to work. What happens then can be seen as a negotiating process, with two possible outcomes: they come to an agreement or not. We will not go into this here, especially as in practice clients do not often disagree with the proposed method.

There are several advantages to this initial clarification. It helps to prevent unfocused chatting. Without a structure both helper and client can easily get the feeling that they have lost control of events. Moreover, the three-stage model encourages the 'common sense' expectation that problems can be solved. The open involvement of the client in the course of events concerns not only the cooperative relationship but also more practical matters such as the duration, the frequency, and perhaps even the cost of these sessions. In summary it can be said that the client should first of all be adequately informed on what he can expect, but also should himself clearly state his expectations. When these two matters have been discussed the basis for an initial contract has been laid.

After a discussion of the cooperation mode! the initiative shifts to the client, who gets the opportunity to say why he has come. Even when the initiative has been shifted, it is important that the client feels at ease, particularly as he will often be somewhat tense and uncertain. In what way can the helper put the client at ease? In the first place he can pay attention to what the client has to say and show that he is listening to him. The way in which he can do this will be discussed in the next section. In the second place he can show calm and patience in his style of behaviour: 'we have plenty of time'.

The start of an interview can often be somewhat tense, especially with a new to counselling helper. 'What kind of person am I dealing with?' is his thought. This tension can be relieved by concentrating on one's breathing and relaxing by breathing deeply a few times. More important, though, is the right mental attitude, which can be characterized as tolerance of uncertainty. By that we mean that the helper must *know* that – certainly at the beginning of a contact – many questions will remain unanswered and he should accept this with the confidence that he will be able to rectify this later on.

To approach a person with problems in this way is in marked contrast to what often happens in daily life. Someone has a problem: we comfort him, suggest all kinds of solutions, appease him, say that it is not his fault, and that the problem occurs very often, etc. Listening quietly to a problem is difficult and even more so when as an 'expert' one believes one is expected to find a solution quickly.

'Non'-selective listening skills, attending behaviour

Nearly every reader will have had the following experience. When you come back from a holiday and want to talk about it, you find you have very little to say to one person, whereas with another your story will get attention and you feel encouraged to talk at some length. This has everything to do with the way people listen. Some people are past masters at interrupting and going into irrelevant details. You soon lose the desire to go on with your account. You think, 'Oh well, forget it!' What also frequently happens in such a situation is that the listener 'takes over' the conversation. He has also experienced what you are trying to tell him, and more so. This attitude does not encourage you to go on with your story.

But what do the people who encourage you to tell your story actually do? They demonstrate a willingness to pay attention, and show they are interested without wanting immediately to jump in and tell you their own experiences or opinions. This makes them good listeners. But what exactly is a 'good' listener?

Nearly everyone knows that you can listen with great fascination to someone, to the extent of 'forgetting yourself'. When you have listened attentively to a story, have watched a movie or a football game, you have briefly 'forgotten yourself'. For that reason such events can be very relaxing.

It seems as if we are saying: 'When a helper is really interested in a client, he should forget himself and direct all his attention to the client, he should lose himself in the client.' But the snag is that when you 'forget yourself', or 'lose yourself' you are no longer conscious of what you are doing, which means that you may then also do things which on further analysis are found to be not very sensible.

We must therefore make a distinction between a friend who listens attentively to a holiday account and a helper who listens attentively to a client, although when we consider the concrete behaviour in both cases, important similarities are evident. The difference is this. With a friend, uninhibited, unreflective attention can do no harm; it may even be the most pleasant kind of attention imaginable. He loses himself in you, he is all ears! The helper should also be all ears, but his attentive attitude should not be unreflective, he must not forget himself. Why not? In the first place because 'spontaneous' utterances can have a positive, but also a negative effect on the course of the conversation. Such a helper is capable of making the same mistakes we mentioned above: going into irrelevant details, interruptions, etc. In the second place because the helper must be able to justify his conduct to his professional peer group. Thus the helper has to consider everything he does, including the giving of attention.

This reflective attention should, nevertheless, resemble real, spontaneous attention by very sensitively keeping under control certain behaviours which one is not usually aware of in ordinary conversation. Which behaviours are meant here?

We will deal first with several non-verbal and verbal aspects. Watzlawick, Beavin, and Jackson (1967) distinguish between the content and the relational aspect of communication. The content aspect concerns the actual information that is communicated. The relational aspect refers to the relation between the communicating parties as this is expressed. The relational aspect is made clear by non-verbal signals and intonation. We will demonstrate this with an example.

When Mary says to John, 'John, would you close the door', she can express very different things. She can pronounce this remark in a servile, ordering, loving, or sarcastic manner. From her intonation and facial expression can be inferred how Mary at that moment defines her 'relation' to John. The way in which John then looks upon this relation will largely determine the nature of his response.

In counselling a distinction can also be made between what is said – the content aspect – and how it is said – the relational aspect. This may refer to what the client says about his relations with others, though it can also concern the relation between helper and client. In the following section the main issue will be the attitude shown by the helper to his client. We will therefore first discuss some non-verbal behaviours which can show his attention and interest. These aspects are important. According to Mehrabian (1972), about half of all communication takes place through these non-verbal channels. The helper will have to realize that the relational aspect, apart from the behaviour of the client opposite him, is also present in his own communicative behaviour.

Non-verbal behaviour

Facial expression

Someone's facial expression can immediately communicate whether he is interested in what the other is telling him or whether his thoughts are on other things. The helper's facial expression is as meaningful to the client as that of the client to the helper. He may find this expression stimulating or inhibiting.

The face is the primary site for communication of emotional states. It reflects interpersonal attitudes; it provides non-verbal feedback on the comments of others; and some say it is the primary source of information next to human speech.

(Knapp 1978: 263)

Facial expressions are a highly significant means of communication, more significantly and directly linked to emotions and intentions than one often realizes. The most remarkable facial expression, according to Hackney and Cormier (1979) is the smile. It can express interest, benevolence, and sympathy, which can be very stimulating. However, the dosage is very important: any excess may result in the client feeling that he is not being taken seriously. Frequent or constant frowning can be taken as a sign of disapproval. However, an occasional frown can indicate to the client that the helper is doing his best to understand him. In that case it shows involvement and may lead to the client being encouraged to greater elucidation.

'The face is the mirror of the soul.' This is also true of the helper. The 'soul' contains the basic demeanour of acceptance and interest. People are often unaware of their facial expression, although this does not mean that it cannot be controlled. Which expression is used depends on the situation. When somebody tells a good joke, people laugh spontaneously; when something sad occurs they look serious. That people can manipulate their facial expression can be concluded from the fact that one can, for example, dutifully laugh or look serious.

As helpers we should monitor our facial expressions. In Chapter 3 we spoke of 'genuineness' and said that the helper does not have to show the client everything he thinks or feels. His face can betray him, however, and he will have to take that into account to avoid incongruency in his behaviour.

When the helper thinks, 'How boring this is', he should be aware of this thought and also of the fact that the attendant bored look on his face will not be very encouraging to his client. He can choose one of two strategies to deal with this. First, he can consciously manipulate and control his expression. This action is to be preferred in those situations where he does not think it appropriate to reveal what he 'really' feels. Or he may let his facial expression show what he is feeling. He then 'really' looks bored or irritated. He should realize, though, that the sending of such a non-verbal message alone is not very explicit and may possibly confuse and upset the client. Hence it is better to give an explanation of his bored look, for instance: 'Yes, you probably notice that I am looking a little bored; that is because I'm wondering if you are not wandering off the track.' Such a response can be characterized as 'directness' (see also p. 154). The client then knows what the matter is and why the helper is looking bored.

The helper should not, of course, pay constant attention to the expression on his face – that is likely to make him appear rather artificial. Rather, his main attention should be directed to the client. It is important, however, that he should be conscious from time to time of the possible effects of his facial expression.

Looking

Appropriate looking means that the helper looks at, or in the direction of, the client for most of the time, and occasionally makes eye contact. This does not mean he should overdo the looking and stare, but neither should it be entirely avoided. The former can lead to the client becoming anxious: 'Why is he watching me in that penetrating way?' he may think. In this case the client will have the unpleasant sensation of being studied. 'He does not talk to me; he studies me.' On the other hand, avoidance of looking results in the client feeling that the helper is not really involved.

Body language

The helper's attention can also be expressed in a relaxed, sympathetic posture. Such a posture also makes it easier for him to listen attentively. The effect on the client is that he, too, will also feel more relaxed. A relaxed helper inspires more confidence than either a tense one or one who is moving and gesturing. 'Fidgeting' is easily associated by the client with nervousness. The point here is that it is more pleasant for somebody who is rather agitated to talk to a person who radiates a certain calm and stability.

Encouraging gestures

By nodding and supportive hand gestures, as well as by the absence of nervous, distracting movements, the helper can also express his attention and encourage the client to continue talking.

Verbal following

Another 'non'-selective way to show attention is to follow the client verbally. This means that the helper ensures that his comments link up as closely as possible with what the client says and do not introduce new topics. To follow closely verbally what a client is saying gives the client the opportunity to explore and elaborate his own line of thought. This activity alone – to formulate out loud one's problems and anxieties to a listening other party – can have a clarifying effect. In order to follow the client the helper should set aside his own (interpreting) thoughts and try to project himself into the client's situation.

What is 'verbal following' specifically? The least selective form is the response we call 'minimal encouragement'.

Minimal encouragements are brief verbal responses intended to encourage the client and show that he is being listened to. Examples of minimal encouragements are: 'hm,hm'; 'yes'; 'oh?'; 'and then?'; 'go on'; or the repetition of one or two words in an inquiring tone of voice. These interjections which at first sight seem to be rather insignificant, are in practice a great help in encouraging the client to go on talking (Greenspoon 1955). For example:

Client: Well, after a lot of talking back and forth it turned into an enormous fight. . . .
Helper: A fight, you say?
Client: Yes indeed, he started throwing things and finally he left the house very angrily. . . .
Helper: Hm, hm, and then?
Client: I got into a panic. I thought he would never come back. . . .
Helper: Hm, hm. . . .
Client: Well, I was wrong about that, thankfully. An hour later he was back, but it has made us think.
Helper: In what way?

In the example we see that the helper needs very few words to let the client tell her story. What he says always links up with what the client has just said. By using minimal encouragements the helper shows that he is interested and invites her to continue talking. At the beginning of a counselling session minimal encouragements often suffice to keep the client's story going.

Silences

A brief silence can also be a sign of encouragement, since it gives the client the opportunity to consider quietly what he has just said and what he may want to add to that. Hackney and Cormier (1979) distinguish between silences induced by the helper and those caused by the client. We deliberately used the word 'brief' silence, for a distinction should be made between the silence controlled by the helper and the unduly long, uncontrolled silence that may bring the conversation to a halt. In the latter case the client may start to think, 'Now even the helper does not know what to say. What's wrong with me?' These kinds of silence are rightly called embarrassing.

When the client falls silent there may be three possible grounds for this.

1 The first and most positive ground is that he is busy processing something; he may, for example, be considering ways to tackle the problem he has just described.
2 The second reason is that he finds it difficult to continue talking. Some subjects may be so emotionally burdened that the client is afraid to go on. We may also encounter avoidance behaviour here: to go on talking sometimes means confessing to your own foolishness or doubts. That is scary. You only dare to do this when you completely trust the helper.
3 A third reason is that the client simply does not know what else he should say or do.

It is up to the helper to assess the kind of silence. Usually this assessment is possible from the context of the conversation. When he finds it hard to judge why the client is silent for such a long period, he can ask him. For example:

Helper: I notice that you have been quiet for some time. Why do you think that is so?

This has the effect of opening the issue of the silence to discussion (see also Situation clarification, p. 124).

When we take a close look at the three aforementioned reasons for silence, the client will in the first case answer the question something like:

Client: Well, I was thinking about a way I might improve my relationship with my husband.

With a reaction like this the helper should aim at a further exploration of the thoughts thus expressed. In the second case, when the client has trouble continuing, she will probably be less quick to respond. Her response may even be a little hesitant.

Client: Well, eh, you see . . . I don't really know if I should say this, but . . . I think it is really crazy but eh . . . I really never loved my husband. We got married more because it was the thing to do.

Precisely this hesitant, stumbling way of talking should put the helper on his guard: 'This is a hot topic.' In this kind of situation particularly, he must create an atmosphere of security, show the client that he does not condemn her, however crazy this may be, or rather, however crazy the client believes it to be. To show understanding ('I understand that you find it difficult to talk about this') is a precondition to a further discussion of the problem.

In the third case the client will say something like:

Client: I don't know what else to tell you, I think I have said everything I can think of.

The helper's response here will depend on the situation. When he agrees with the client that the whole story has been told, he will start on his summary (see p. 120). When he thinks that certain parts of the problem still need further elucidation, he will say so and ask for more information and concretization (see p. 116).

A retrospective view

By making use of the non-verbal and verbal skills discussed so far, the helper can create a situation in which the client need not feel threatened since he knows he is in contact with someone who pays attention to him and does not immediately come forward with his own ideas.

This skill of listening and paying attention is often considered not only natural but also easy. Certainly it comes more easily when the helper has the right underlying attitude of giving total attention. However, even then ordinary habit patterns are sometimes difficult to change. As an unexperienced counsellor on one course said, 'I really mean to listen, but I now see (on the videotape) that I did not do so.' Our experience is that helpers new to counselling, in particular, are so eager to help and feel so strongly that they should do something for their client quickly, that they often cannot muster the patience to listen first, with the result that they tend to ask a lot of questions in order to find a swift solution. Consequently, the client is given little space. Another frequently occurring phenomenon is that the helper, when hearing the problems, himself has thought-associations relating to similar experiences. He 'recognizes' the story: 'Ah, I've heard that before', or, 'Hey, I've had that too'. It is then very hard to suppress the inclination to think that 'this will probably be exactly the same' and ask questions from that viewpoint.

In the training courses we conducted such 'beginner's mistakes' proved to be the rule rather than the exception. It was found necessary not so much to teach the students 'listening behaviour' as to 'unlearn' all kinds of conversational habits acquired in daily life. In this connection it is also clear why 'ordinary' conversations, in which somebody tries to talk only about his problems, are often so frustrating for the person concerned. Either the listener is too eager to help or he does not feel like it, does not know what to do about it, or is afraid of it. In all cases there is a tendency to respond too quickly.

In order to clarify the above we will close this section with two brief interview extracts. In the first we see a helper who, despite his good intentions, does not listen well to the client. In the second case we let the same client speak once more, but now with a skilled helper listening.

1 *Helper:* Hello, Mrs X. You have made an appointment to come and talk. Tell me a bit about why you have come?
  Client: I have so many problems at work.
2 *Helper:* What kind of work do you do?
  Client: I am a teacher.
3 *Helper:* Hm,hm. . . .
  Client: Well, you see, I haven't had this job very long, it takes me ages to prepare my lessons and I hardly have any time for myself . . . .
4 *Helper:* Are you good at keeping order?
  Client: Well, that's not so bad really, of course in the beginning it is not so easy, but. . . .
5 *Helper:* No, no, so that is not exactly the problem.
  Client: No, I don't think so.
6 *Helper:* What subject do you teach?
  Client: French.

7 *Helper:* Well, of course that's not the easiest subject there is, and the children are perhaps not very motivated?
Client: Oh, that's not so bad really, but maybe it also plays a part . . . .
8 *Helper:* What part do you think it plays?
Client: Well, perhaps it makes me a bit tense. . . .
9 *Helper:* Can you discuss this with your colleagues? After all, they are more experienced than you are.
Client:[slightly irritated] Well . . . I do not like them all equally well, but I don't think that that's the problem. . . .

When we analyse this interview we see that the helper fails mainly in the 'verbal following' of his client. He does not link up with what she tells him, but is testing out his own hypothesis. This takes place right from the beginning. After his first question he wants to know quickly what *kind* of work his client does, whereas the client wants to talk about *the problems* at work. It is understandable and probably also necessary that he wants to know that, but would he not have found out anyway?

Another example is intervention 4 ('Are you good at keeping order?') and 5 ('No, no, so that is not exactly the problem.'). The helper then continues with his investigation, without letting the client say what she thinks. With intervention 7 we see the helper put forward his own idea about the problem. The client doubts this but bends to his authority: '. . . maybe it also plays a part'. The helper thinks he is on to something! He has discovered the root of the problem, he thinks. With intervention 8 we see the helper following up this idea of his. But still the client is given some space with an open question. With intervention 9 the helper again comes from his own frame of reference, again showing that he is busy looking for solutions ('Can you discuss this with your colleagues?'). He is badly amiss here, with the result that the client becomes irritated. This is not surprising, for she feels misunderstood (where she may have expected understanding), and feels that she is not being given the opportunity to tell her story.

In summary we can say that the way in which this interview is conducted shows a lack of direction. The reason may be that the helper is not very tolerant of uncertainty and wants to give answers to all the questions. It may also be that he thinks his own ideas are very important. Whatever the reason, the process of problem clarification is laborious. Is there another way? Let us see.

1 *Helper:* Hello, Mrs X. You have made an appointment to come and talk. Tell me a bit about why you have come?
Client: I have so many problems at work. . . .

2 *Helper:* Hm, hm.
Client: Well, you see, I work in a high school and I haven't done this for very long, so I need a lot of time to prepare my lessons and I hardly have any time left for myself.

3 *Helper:* What do you mean . . . time left for yourself?
Client: Well, I used to do a lot of things just for pleasure, but I hardly have time for that any more. I am busy with nothing but school, I sometimes wonder if I'm heading for a nervous breakdown. . . .

4 *Helper:* [Looks and attends but remains silent]
Client: I hardly sleep a wink at night. Everything keeps going through my head. And then I get up very early to go over all my lessons once again, because I'm worried that I won't have everything organized next day.

5 *Helper:* [Pause] Tell me a bit more about that?
Client: Well, uh, I think that things can't go on like this. I may be exaggerating, every beginning is difficult, of course, but still. . . .

6 *Helper:* But still?
Client: It is not good . . . when I see how my lessons go, I cannot really complain. . . .

7 *Helper:* How do you mean?
Client: Well, in most classes I can keep order all right, but the dean, you know. . . .

8 *Helper:* The dean?
Client: Yes, I have the feeling that he doesn't have much confidence in me, and I still don't have a permanent appointment, so. . . .

9 *Helper:* So?
Client: So I worry about that. I can't bear to think that maybe next year I will be out of a job.

When we compare this fragment with the preceding one, we are struck first of all by the fact that the helper links up directly with what the client tells him. This gives her space to determine the content and direction of the dialogue. We also see that the effect of this 'verbal following' is that quite different and probably more relevant information is brought forward by the client (her insomnia, her fear of a nervous breakdown, the relation with the dean which may have consequences for the permanent appointment).

All the interventions are in the form of 'minimal encouragements'. Instead of being irritated the client responds with more and more disclosures. She feels understood and continues with her story. Nowhere does the helper show a tendency to search for solutions. That is uncalled for at this stage, for if solutions were easy and quick to find, the client would very likely already have thought of them herself.

Is it therefore a good thing to keep on following the client indefinitely? Certainly not! For then there is a chance that both helper and client will get bogged down. To prevent this happening a more active attitude may be required of the helper. And this brings us to the next section.

Selective listening skills

Apart from 'non'-selective skills the helper should also employ selective skills. Before making a distinction between various separate skills we will first take a closer look at the concept of 'selectivity'. What is meant by that? Selectivity refers first of all to the fact that the helper in his interventions may pay more attention to certain aspects of the client's story than to others. This can be done by going more deeply either into the *content* or the *feeling*. Another way is to give extra attention to a certain *subject*.

In the following paragraphs we will first discuss the separate selective skills and subsequently the selection of subjects to be discussed.

Asking questions

In the first phase of a counselling interview the object of asking questions is to help the client to put his thoughts into words and clarify his problems. We make a significant distinction here between *open* and *closed* questions.

Open questions
Open questions leave the client a considerable amount of freedom in the formulation of his answer. It means that he can express in his own

words what is on his mind. In other words, he can talk from his own frame of reference and determine for himself the direction and content of the conversation.

A simple but effective way to put good open questions is to begin them with: 'How?', 'What?', or 'Can you tell me something about ... ?' With these open questions we can differentiate between the amount of space offered. Compare the following questions:

- What is on your mind?
- What brings you here?
- What is it you want to talk about?
- How are things at work?
- What do you think you can do about your problem?
- Can you tell me about your daily schedule?

With the first three questions both the content and the form of the response are unrestrained. The only restriction is that the client should talk. The last three questions offer less space because they refer to a certain area (work, problems, daily schedule) but within that area the client is free to turn in any direction.

The helper can use *open questions* at various points:

a   At the *beginning* of an interview, for example: *'How* can I help?' or: *'How* did things go during the past week?'
b   *During* the interview, for instance when he does not quite understand the client or wants to know more about a certain *subject*, as in: *'What* do you mean by that?' or: 'Can you tell me a little more about the relation with your parents?'

A distinction can also be made between open questions *connected* to what the client has said and open questions relating to a *new* subject. Open questions of the connecting kind can be asked when the helper wants to know more about something which has already been discussed and/or when he wants to encourage the client to explore a subject further. He may ask open questions on a new subject when – in his own or in both their opinions – a given subject has been sufficiently discussed. Open questions may also refer to a special subject selected by the helper. The following series of open questions serves as an example:

- How's life in general?
- How are things at work?

- What kind of a job do you have?
- How do you broach the subject of salaries with your boss?
- What did your boss think of your suggestion that you were not earning enough?

In this series of questions the field of inquiry is narrowed down more and more and the information obtained is more precise, but the possibility of the client deciding himself on the answer is kept open.

Closed (direct) questions

With this type of question the answer is determined largely by the content of the question. Generally the person answering can simply give a confirmation or denial. Examples of closed questions are:

- Are you all right?
- Have you had this long?
- Are you married?
- Do you visit your parents often?
- Was your mother angry when you came back?
- Did you go to see him right away when you heard that?

It is clear that the person to whom the questions are directed can confine himself to very brief answers. Closed questions often stem from the helper's frame of reference. This has several drawbacks. One of them is that it restricts the client in his range of possible responses. A second is that such questions, stemming from a certain preconceived notion, are often suggestive. For example:

Client: I have been sleeping badly lately.
Helper: Is that because you have been too busy?

From this question it appears that the helper himself has a suspicion concerning the cause of the sleeplessness; this suspicion results in exploration of this idea. This directed exploration is contrary to the goal of keeping to the client's frame of reference. The degree of suggestiveness, however, depends very much on the *tone* in which the helper puts his question. 'Could it have anything to do with the fact that you are so busy at the moment?' already sounds considerably less suggestive. The degree to which the client will be inclined to agree with the suggestion depends also on his suggestibility. The helper should be aware of the fact that the client may sometimes attach greater significance to the helper's (suggestive) questions than is desirable.

A third disadvantage of closed questions is the effect that they may have on the course of the conversation. The result is that the client feels less responsible for the discussion. This may result in the client giving ever shorter answers, after which it is up to the helper to think of new questions. Apart from the fact that in this way the conversation will increasingly start to look like a cross-examination, the helper will eventually get stuck himself, since he has run out of questions to ask. This does not help to produce a relaxed atmosphere.

When open and when closed questions?

When asking questions a helper has several possibilities to choose from. His choice should depend mainly on the goal he has in mind. When he wants to give the client space and wants to hear what the latter thinks is important (and this is the case in the problem clarification stage) it is best to ask *open* questions; when he wants to know specifics or wants to check whether he has understood the story up to now, it is better to ask *closed* (direct) questions.

Precise rules for the use of open and closed questions cannot be given here. In principle the helper should have both types of question in his repertoire, so that he can vary them during the conversation as he sees fit.

Why-questions

The why-questions deserve separate mention. In its form the why-question is an open one, which sometimes can be quite adequate. After all, people often have a motive for doing something; moreover, they often have a personal theory about (the origin of) their problems. On the other hand such questions, especially at the beginning of the contact, can appear to be quite threatening. The client may get the idea that he is being asked to justify himself, whereas the point of the conversation is that he can explore his thoughts and feelings. When he is forced to give explanations ('Why do you have problems?') about matters on which he is not very clear himself, there is also a chance that he will get confused. Thus in certain cases the why-question will only lead to feigned answers or to defensiveness.

We want to stress once more the importance of the *tone* in which such a question is asked. This can give a question a double meaning, for example not only inviting an explanation ('Do you have any idea why you drink so much?') but also implying a criticism, calling the client to account ('Why do you drink so much?').

Paraphrasing of content

The second selective listening skill we will discuss is 'paraphrasing of content'. This means: *briefly reproducing in one's own words* the gist of what the client has said. The main characteristic of the paraphrase is that it refers to the information content of the client's responses. This information may relate to events, persons or things (Hackney and Cormier 1979). This listening skill is important in that it demonstrates to the client a genuine interest, acceptance and understanding (see Chapter 3). When the helper demonstrates his attention only by means of the skills discussed up to now, such as his posture, his eye contact, his minimal encouragements, and his questions, the conversation may remain somewhat sterile. Although the client sees and notices that the helper is listening, he does not hear it, he does not really get the feeling 'Yes, he really understands me!' Thus the paraphrase gives a 'translation' of the essence of what the client has said.

The use of this skill has several purposes:

1 The client realizes that he is being listened to, and it can be refreshing and stimulating for him to hear his own story again but worded differently. This requires from the helper a certain flexibility in the use of language to capture nuances of meaning. A literal repetition of the client's words may sound ridiculous.

2 The helper finds out whether he has understood the client correctly; this is especially useful when the client's account contains much complex or confusing information. For instance:

Client: So we were on holiday in France. I was there with my wife, the children and another couple, friends of ours. But quite suddenly everything seemed to go wrong. My wife was nagging the whole time, we quarrelled with the other couple and on top of that my son got sick. I think that holiday made me more tired than my work.

Helper: If I understand you correctly, a lot of quite unpleasant things happened during your holiday, so bad even that you did not really get any rest at all.

Client: Yes, indeed and .... [etc.]

3 Apart from these goals (to show understanding and/or to
check whether the story has been understood) the goal can
also be to reproduce what the client has said more precisely,
thereby giving the client a clearer picture of his problems.

In the example above the helper *selects* the tiredness of the client
as the item on which to focus attention. In social learning theory
terms, we have here a *selective reinforcement* of a certain part of the
client's story to the neglect of other parts. Thus in the example the
helper does not pursue the following subjects: 1. the wife's nagging;
2. the quarrel with his friends; 3. the illness of his son. These topics
are ignored for the time being. It is a question of careful choice and
judgement as to which aspects of the client's story the helper pays
most attention to. He can usually deduce from the client's way of
talking what he thinks is most important. This he can do by listening
keenly to the things stressed most by the client or said with the greatest hesitation. The tone of voice is often very significant here.

When applying this skill it is important for the helper to be aware
of his own preconceptions and not confuse these with what the client
says. When he believes he already knows what is the matter, because
'such things are always like that', the helper runs the risk of expressing in his paraphrase his own preconceived ideas rather than 'return-
ing' the client's own words. In this connection it is also important
that the paraphrases are said in a *tentative tone of voice*. This gives the
client an opportunity and invitation to correct the helper when he is
not entirely accurate. It is necessary to give this opportunity for correction, since someone in trouble is often vulnerable, insecure, and
in awe of the helper, and may end up saying what he thinks the helper
wants him to say.

In this section we have discussed the helper's response to the *content* of the client's account. This content should be distinguished
from the *feelings* involved, though it is often difficult to make a sharp
distinction. The two aspects frequently overlap. In the choice of response, however, a distinction can usefully be made between paraphrasing content and reflecting feelings. By paraphrasing, the content aspects are stressed, whereas a reflection places greater emphasis on the emotional side. We now turn to this latter skill.

Reflection of feeling

'Reflection of feeling' literally means the reproducing or mirroring of feeling. The helper can respond in two ways to the client's story: either he stresses the factual aspects – the content – or the more emotional aspects. By paraphrasing the content the helper shows that he is trying to understand *what* the client says about himself or his present or past situation. By reflecting feeling he demonstrates that he is trying to understand *how* the client *feels* during the conversation or *has felt* in the situation he is describing. This can be of paramount importance. From the tone in which people speak can often be inferred what they mean. When he is reflecting feelings the helper abstains from giving his own value judgement, but shows mainly understanding. This skill in particular is an important concrete manifestation of empathy. Its first function is to show the client that his feelings, of whatever nature, are understood and accepted and are worthy of attention. He senses that someone is sitting there who can put himself in his experiencing world. As a result he is encouraged to express his feelings and to be more aware of them. Moreover, this acceptance gives the client a greater sense of security and the courage to express with greater ease feelings which he himself may find hard to accept. As such the reflection of feeling contributes to the general goal: problem clarification. The last function of reflection is (just as with paraphrasing) a control function: the helper checks whether with his reflection he has assessed the client's feelings correctly. When he is not sure if he is on the right track with his reflection, the helper should use a tentative tone. But when the client's feelings are very obvious, for example when he is furious about a certain event, a confirming tone in the reflection is more suitable.

In order to demonstrate the difference between paraphrasing content and reflecting feeling, we will give a few examples.

Example 1

Client: When we were at that party, my husband was terrible. He had drunk a lot again, he annoyed the other guests and when I finally said that I wanted to go home, he slapped me in the face!

Helper: [Paraphrase] When you were at that party, your husband behaved very badly towards you and the others.
[Reflection]:You were furious with your husband.

Example 2

Client: I really don't know what to do when I finish school. There are so many possibilities.

Helper: [Paraphrase] You are having difficulty making a choice.
[Reflection] You are full of doubts.

Example 3

Client: A lot has happened since we last met. I have had a talk with my father and he was not angry at all!

Helper: [Paraphrase] So, you have talked with you father and it went well.
[Reflection] So, what a relief for you!

With the paraphrase we see that the helper mainly discusses the content of what has been said, while with his reflections he responds to the underlying emotional tone. But the helper can in his response to the client also combine a paraphrase with a reflection. For example, in response to example 1:

Helper: With your husband behaving and finally even slapping you [Paraphrase], you must have got really mad at him [Reflection].

How well the helper reflects feelings depends largely on his ability to recognize and be sensitive to moods. Clients may show in various ways how they feel or have felt. They may show it directly with (emotional) words, such as: 'I am afraid, I was disappointed, I was content, I am enthusiastic', but more frequently in a non-verbal manner, by talking quickly, by the loudness of voice, the intonation, the muscle tension, posture, blushing, lowering of the eyes. All these phenomena can be taken as expressions of the emotional state. By being alert to these behaviours the helper can assist the client in further exploration of his feelings.

Feelings can be divided into those that are simple or complex. Simple feelings can be positive ('I was/am glad') or negative ('I was/am sad'). Complex feelings, though, are often confusing and they occur especially in emotional situations. In the example described above the woman may have been not only angry but also ashamed. Someone who has broken off a long-lasting relationship can be both sad and relieved. Feelings of tension can simultaneously be positive and negative. When these feelings occur in a client, it is particularly

113

important that the helper shows his understanding and obviously does not think it odd that there is an interplay between various feelings, positive as well as negative.

Another distinction we want to make concerns the subject of feelings: feelings the client has for himself, feelings with regard to other persons or an event, and feelings toward the helper. For instance, a person may be disappointed in himself, be enthusiastic about a football match, and have feelings of inferiority in relation to the helper.

A final differentiation can be made between feelings the client has now, at the present time, and feelings he had in the past. With the woman in the example the anger may emerge once more during the telling ('You are still angry about it!'), or she can talk about it with a certain distance ('You were very angry at the time').

When applying this skill it is important to be fully in touch with the client, in so far as the feelings expressed by the client are reflected with equal intensity. When someone says, for example: 'I feel so listless', a reflection: 'So you do not enjoy life any longer' is, as far as intensity is concerned, much too strong, while 'You are a little bored' is far too weak. Moreover, the reflection should correspond to the nature of the emotion expressed. This seems obvious, but in practice it is found to be far from simple. We have developed a number of fragments of interviews on videocassette for training purposes, in which something is said in a certain tone of voice. The purpose of these fragments is to train the skill 'reflection of feeling' separately. The instruction to the students is to decode and reflect for each fragment the underlying feeling (see Appendix I, Videotapes). It sometimes happens that 'pride' is mistaken for 'indifference' and vice versa. When the helper is a little off course this by no means need have immediate disastrous consequences. It may even contribute to a more exact definition of the client's words. For example:

Client: When my mother called me all sorts of bad things because in her eyes I had again done something wrong, well, I thought: I don't care any more!

Helper: You got very angry?

Client: Well, I wasn't angry so much as indifferent, in the sense that: from now on I will decide for myself what I think is right and what is not and I don't care one bit what you think!

The important thing is that the client notices that the helper is trying to understand him and that he accepts him. It becomes embarrassing, of course, when in his reflections the helper continues to be off course. Then the client gets the feeling that he really doesn't understand at all.

Reflection of feeling is often found to be one of the hardest skills to master. In the first place the *recognition* of feelings leads to problems. It is difficult to pay attention to something said 'between the lines' instead of explicitly. A second difficulty lies in the fact that in daily life emotions are often experienced as threatening and are not expressed directly. When it does happen, it is often not followed by any reaction; it is apparently tempting to *ignore* emotions. Why should that be so? Apart from the fact that in ordinary conversation the trend is 'not to be difficult', it is also possible that people are afraid of someone else's emotions, since they make him come (too) close (see Michael's friend in Chapter 2). When someone says that he is often depressed, it may be that we realize that this is also true of ourselves, but that we would rather not let the other person know about it. It is also possible that we do not quite know how to respond to such a statement. At any rate, in our culture people often prefer to discuss the factual aspects of a problem and to avoid the emotional ones.

Are we saying that in ordinary life feelings should be discussed more openly, that people should respond more to each other's feelings? We do not want to give a value judgement on that. Everyone must decide this for himself. But there are two extremes which we think are both undesirable. On the one side we have people who never express any emotion, but who rationalize everything; on the other side there are those who talk about their feelngs at each and every opportunity.

As far as we are concerned, in daily life it is everybody's privilege to respond to someone else's feelings or not. With regard to the helper, however, we are of the opinion that he should be capable of using the skill of 'reflection of feeling'. In counselling it is a question of tackling problems, of doing something about them and not of ignoring them. In ordinary conversation people often evade problems. In our role as helper we have to give up that habit. With mental problems the emotional component plays a most important part after all. To acknowledge and show understanding of the client's feelings is also a condition for gaining his trust. That trust is vital for fruitful cooperation and that, in turn, is necessary to achieve the goal of problem clarification and finally an effective treatment of the problem.

Concreteness

An important skill in the stage of problem clarification is 'concreteness': to help the client be as accurate and precise as possible when discussing his problems. Concreteness is a composite skill in the sense that the skills mentioned above – listening, encouraging, open and closed questions, paraphrasing, and reflecting – all contribute to it. By merely listening and encouraging, the helper can stimulate the client to give a detailed rendition of the problem. When that is not sufficient, the client's response to specific open and closed questions can create greater clarity. Finally, paraphrases and reflections may also enhance the accuracy and specificity of the problem's description. In order to let the client tell his story as concretely as possible, the helper too, will have to be concrete and differentiated in his use of language (Egan 1975, 1982). After all, the helper is also providing a model for the client.

The purpose of this skill is that the client achieves greater precision with regard to his problem. In ordinary daily life we often neglect to do this:

How are you?
I'm fine.
That's good.

What exactly is 'fine' does not usually interest us that much. In the relation with the client with a problem, however, we should not be satisfied so easily, for the client is then not encouraged to describe his problem in detail, while the helper will probably not get a clear picture of the problems. This detailed rendering of the story is important to both of them, since it contributes to a sharper and more differentiated view of the problematic situation (see p. 36). Moreover, it is often a pleasant experience for the client that the helper is also interested in seemingly irrelevant detail. That gives him the feeling: 'My story is important, I am being taken seriously, he is paying attention to me,' or: 'At last, somebody who really wants to know everything, someone who wants to know what I think.'

Many people, including helpers – especially those who have been counselling for a longer period (Wills 1978) – tend too readily to assume that they understand other people's stories and problems, based on their experience with 'comparable problems'. But by adopting this attitude they disregard the uniqueness of people and their experiences. To 'understand' problems too readily may also result in unfounded advice being given.

Another reason why clear definitions are important is that clients are often inclined to wrap up their problems in vague and abstract terms. One reason for this may be that 'to call a spade a spade' is felt to be threatening; to keep one's experiences abstract and vague reduces this anxiety. Another explanation is that many people are not used to expressing themselves in terms of specific details: 'Everything's gone wrong', 'That's the way it is', etc.

The helper who responds to such vague words only with reflections or paraphrases enhances the obscurity. Merely saying: 'You were very scared' is not enough, when the reason why and of what the client is afraid remains unclear. Chomsky (1965, 1968) made a distinction between the surface structure and the depth structure of statements. Using these concepts Bandler and Grinder (1975) suggest that it is up to the helper to help the client realize the depth structure of his statements.

Let us illustrate this with an example. In this example the client's vague statements are italicized.

Client [warehouse clerk]: *Everything* seems to be going *badly.*
Helper: What is going badly? Can you tell me a little more about it?
Client: Things are going badly at work.

Here we see the first specification. Things are not going badly on all fronts but concern his work. Thus there is a differentiation in situations. In order to test whether 'it' is also going badly in other fields, the helper could ask: 'Are there other situations in which things are not going very well for you?' The helper, though, first continues with the work situation.

Helper: What exactly is wrong at work?
Client: I cannot get along with my boss.

The contours of the problem situation are becoming clearer, but the helper is not finished yet. What does 'I cannot get along with my boss' mean? Moreover, he may ask himself: 'Do the problems at work only involve the boss, or colleagues as well; or does the client simply not like his job?' He cannot find this out all at once, so he decides to ask a further question.

Helper: That doesn't sound too good. Can you give an example?

Client: He gives me *very little responsibility;* he keeps *nagging* at me *all day.*

The problem is becoming clearer again. But what is 'little reponsibility', how long is 'all day' and what does this 'nagging' consist of? He decides to explore further two vaguenesses.

Helper: What do you mean by 'little responsibility'?
Client: He *checks nearly everything* I do.
Helper: And the 'nagging', how is that expressed?
Client: Well, he *keeps on* criticizing me, that the boxes are not piled up correctly, and that my administration is not up to date; it drives me crazy!

By now the picture that was so obscure at the beginning has been filled in and become sharper. But the helper might continue to define it even more, for instance:

Helper: What do you mean: 'he keeps on'?
or: What do you mean: it 'drives me crazy'?
or: What were your feelings?
or: How often does this happen?
or: What did you think then?

To the discerning reader who now thinks the helper is really interrogating the client, we want to say that the helper might have saved himself some trouble by clearly explaining his motives at the beginning, for instance by giving the following explanation (after the first response): 'Now tell me what exactly is wrong with your work; the more precisely you tell me that, the greater the chance that together we will find out what is the matter' (see also p. 124, Situation clarification). However, not every client has the ability to respond to such a request with a clearcut exposition. It is often necessary for the helper to guide him by asking definite questions, such as used in the example.

Words which should immediately alert the helper to vaguenesses are: 'it', 'always', 'everything', 'never'. Or in general undefined or generalizing statements, such as 'Everything is wrong.' In the example we saw that there was something vague in nearly every phrase used by the client. Specifying makes a client realize that the statement 'Everything seems to be going badly' should only refer to part of his life, namely the relation with his boss.

A client's life is built up not only around different situations but also around a time sequence. He also has a personal history. Specifying questions can also refer to that dimension. We can distinguish between antecedents and consequences.

Helper: Do you have any idea when and how that came about? [Antecedents]
Helper: How do you think this will continue? [Consequences]

The reader may wonder how far one should go with this specification process. Though details are useful, one can be too concrete in the sense that the client is allowed to digress about all kinds of irrelevancies. Therefore we believe that specifications should be used economically. For example, when someone is talking about his holiday and he says, 'It was quite nice', we are dealing with one end of the vagueness spectrum: the general and rather nondescript talker. At the other end is the long-winded talker, who does not leave out any detail:

Well, we left at eight-thirty, with all our bags and stuff that we had already loaded into the car the night before. It was not very good weather when we left; in fact, it rained almost the whole of our trip to Leicester, no to Birmingham, if I remember correctly.

The story as told by this person has no end; it can take hours and at the end all the listeners are asleep. Long-winded specifications only land the talker into a morass of details.

Somewhere between the two ends of the spectrum lies an optimum. This optimum is easier to define when one knows the goal one has in mind. The helper should specify as much as is needed to achieve that end. In the problem clarification stage that end is mainly to give a reasonably exact idea of the problems. Anticipating the stage which deals with the treatment of the problem (Chapter 8), a concrete description of the problem is needed to make clear what action should be taken. In the case described above of the warehouse clerk with problems at work this action might be: have a talk with the boss. After that, the boss's behaviour in the problematic situation could be defined. 'What does he do? When? What do you do in return? What would you like to do?'

Summing up, we can say that concreteness can take place with regard to the following aspects:

- The situation.
- The client's behaviour in the situation.
- The client's ideas about the situation.
- The client's feelings about the situation.
- The reactions of others in the situation.
- Antecedents: what preceded the situation.
- Consequences: what happened after the situation in question.

Summarizing

A distinction can be made between a summary of the contents and a summary of feelings. In the former, emphasis lies on the content of the client's story; in the latter, on its emotional aspects. However, in a summary both content and emotion as well as the links between the two are usually represented and it is merely a question of shifting the emphasis. The difference between summaries of content and feeling on the one hand and paraphrases of content and reflections of feeling on the other lies mainly in the fact that, with summaries, statements by the client over a longer period of time are reproduced. The purpose of the summary is to give a structure to what the client has said by ordering the main points in his story. It is obvious that the selectivity of the helper and the strength of his selective memory will play a greater part here than in the previous skills. The chance of forgetfulness or inaccuracy on the part of the helper is also greater in a summary because the amount of information is greater. Therefore it is very important that summaries are given tentatively, thereby giving the client an opportunity to say whether he agrees.

Like paraphrases and reflections the summary has the following functions:

- The helper can see whether he has understood the client correctly.
- It encourages the client to explore his thoughts and feelings further.
- It brings order into the client's account.

The following somewhat lengthier example demonstrates these points:

Client: Things haven't been going well for me lately. You see, I retired six months ago and since then I have gone downhill. I feel listless, I'm bored, I don't feel like doing anything. . . .

Helper: Hm, hm.

Client: Well, now that I don't work any more I don't know what to do with myself. And another thing . . . when I look back over my work I wonder: is that all you've achieved? My wife can't stand it any longer, my grumbling, that is. She doesn't understand me at all. And now she also wants to move because we can no longer afford the rent, but I'm so attached to my little house. Sometimes I think: I wish I was out of it altogether. . . .

Helper: [Summary] If I understand you correctly, there are a few things intermingling here. I will try and put them in some sort of order. [Note that the helper announces that he is going to give a summary. In that way the client knows what he is doing.] Since your retirement you have been pretty bored, while at the same time you also think that you should have done more while you were still working. Then there is the fact that the relationship with your wife isn't going smoothly plus the fact that she wants to move. All these things together make you feel more and more listless; you can't see a solution . . . . Am I right?

Client: Yes, that's right, that's the way it is.

At this point there are several things the helper can do. He can let a silence fall and wait for the client to continue exploring his problematic situation. In that case the summary is not yet being used to give direction and its function is to ensure that the client notices that he is being listened to. Another possibility, though, is for the helper to give more direction by going deeper into one of the three problems mentioned. For example:

Helper: Thus there are three different things, are there not? Your former work, your wife and moving house. I suggest that we first talk a little more about the problem you mentioned first: that you really think you have not achieved enough. Can you tell me a little more about that?

In this example the helper himself chooses to structure the summary from the things said in the interview. His strategy is to discuss first the feelings of failure with regard to the work situation, followed by difficulties in communication with the wife, and finally the third problem of moving. Another possibility, one that gives the client more space, is for the helper not to do the structuring himself but to consult with the client. For instance:

Helper: Those are three different things, aren't they? Which of the three is for you the most important one to discuss first?

Client: Well, what bothers me most of all is that I have trouble communicating with my wife.

Helper: Can you give an example of that?

From the examples we see that the helper's influence on the direction and structure of the interview is considerable. It should be noted that the last example is most in agreement with the cooperation model: how the interview should be continued is a topic for mutual agreement (see also Situation clarification, p. 124).

One point not mentioned yet is that summaries also make it possible for contrasting emotions to be placed adjacent to each other: to see such juxtapositions and to accept contrasting feelings can be very valuable and liberating. Clients often wrongly think that people are allowed only to have logical and consistent ideas and feelings (Mischel 1968; Ellis 1974).

Finally, some remarks about the 'timing' of a summary.

Suitable times for a summary are:

- When the helper feels the need, after a lengthy and/or confused stream of words by the client, to create some order for himself as well as for the client.
- When the client has apparently said everything he believes to be important.
- At the beginning of a new interview, to pick up the thread of the conversation.

Summaries are misplaced when they disrupt the client's story or when they are used as an emergency measure by a helper who lacks the courage to continue.

Regulating skills

One of the main aims of regulating skills is to safeguard order and clarity in the counselling dialogue. On pp. 93–5 we discussed several skills in this category, particularly starting the interview and making an initial contact. We will now deal with a number of skills important for later counselling sessions: goal-setting and goal-evaluation, situation clarification, thinking aloud, and ending the counselling interview.

Goal-setting and goal-evaluation

In this book counselling is viewed as a goal-directed process. Eventually the outcome goal is the solution of problems. Before that goal can be reached, process goals must be set, as discussed in Chapter 5. It is up to the helper to set up, together with his client, realistic process goals. When the client in the problem clarification stage touches on a number of subjects, such as problems after retirement, communication problems with his wife and financial problems (see p. 121), the process goal is to discuss these subjects separately until they have each been sufficiently clarified.

In general the counselling process is no different from other human activities. Someone who plans to build a house without consulting an architect is likely to make a mess of it. However, to make goals and plans in advance does not mean that everything should be arranged in detail. During the construction the architect can make small alterations. He can do this by posing 'goal-evaluation questions': 'What exactly did I want to achieve?' The answer to this question may lead to an adjustment of the original outcome goal.

During the counselling process it is also useful and necessary for the helper to ask such 'goal-evaluation questions'. When in the initial contract the primary goal has been mutually agreed upon to be problem clarification, the question should occasionally be asked how far one has progressed with this goal. This question not only concerns the helper but should also be discussed with the client. For instance:

Helper: Well, Peter, we have been talking for a while and you have told me a number of things. Now, at the beginning we agreed that our first goal should be to try to get a clearer idea of the problems. I wonder how far we've got with that? Do you think things are a little clearer?

In this example we see that the helper refers to the goal set at the beginning and then lets the client be the first to judge to what extent that goal has been reached. After that the helper should also himself look closely at the problems to see if they have indeed become clearer. He should put his views before the client and if both or one of them believes that the goal has not yet been reached, they will decide on further exploration. When both agree that the goal has been reached, they can jointly decide to end the first stage of the counselling process. At the end of that phase the main problems can be summed up, defined as it were, followed by a discussion on how to continue working. This leads to a new contract in which agreements are reached about the next goal to be aimed at (see Chapters 7 and 8).

Situation clarification

The skill 'situation clarification' refers to the ability of the helper to recognize and discuss ambiguities or misunderstandings occurring during the ongoing dialogue and in the relationship between himself and the client. This skill is important in all phases of counselling, but especially when there seems to be a breakdown in the mutual expectations between helper and client. The objective of this skill is, then, to bring about or restore these mutual expectations. To do this, the helper should closely monitor the interaction between himself and the client. As soon as he observes certain ambiguities he has to decide whether they are important enough to be talked about.

This skill 'situation clarification' is more complex than the listening skills, since it concerns a conversation about a conversation. This is also called a *meta-conversation*. In this meta-conversation the original discussion is looked at from a certain distance. We will make this clear by using the following diagram, derived from Kouwer (1973), in which two conversation levels can be distinguished. For an adequate use of this skill it is necessary for the helper to keep an observer's as well as a participant's view of events occurring during the conversation. The complex cognitive task facing him is first of all to listen very carefully, to put himself in the client's position and at the same time

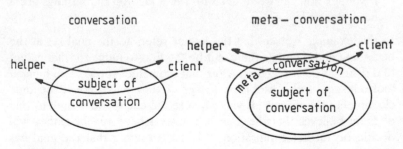

Figure 6.1

to monitor closely what is going on in the discussion, especially in order to identify ambiguities.

To clarify this, we will give a few concrete examples in which an application of this skill is useful.

Example 1

To enter into an initial contract (p. 94) can be viewed as a special form of situation clarification. After all, its function is to achieve the goal of joint cooperation and to clarify everyone's part in this, so that mutual expectations are in tune with each other. An important element in the initial contract is the helper's explanation of the goals and tasks of counselling. It also enables helper and client to agree on the way in which they will work together.

Example 2

A client expects from the helper a quick and fitting solution to his problems. Although the helper has explained her method and has the client's agreement, the former nevertheless often finds that the client still has not entirely understood the situation or wants to persuade the helper to do things differently. The client may still believe that, just like a doctor writing out a prescription, the helper will offer a solution as it were without the client being involved. However, this is not in accordance with the cooperation model (see Chapter 2). We will now demonstrate the function of situation clarification, to solve this problem between helper and client, with the following discussion.

> *Client:* [After ten minutes into the first interview] Well, I think I've told you everything now; my husband appears to be a homosexual and I really can't stand it any longer that he has these contacts with his friend. What should I do now?
> 1 *Helper:* You are wondering how to go on. . . [Paraphrase].
> *Client:* Yes, I really don't know. I think it's awful. All those years he has deceived me. Please tell me: What should I do?
> 2 *Helper:* Yes, I understand you are desperate about that [Reflection], and it is so bad that right now you don't know how to continue and therefore you ask *me:* what in the world should I do. . . [Paraphrase].
> *Client:* [Expectantly] Yes. . . . Yes. . . .
> 3 *Helper:* Well, I think I should say something about that, for I really

don't think I *can* say that right away. In the first place we do not yet have a clear picture of all that is involved here; in the second place I think that even if the picture has become clear it is better if we look *together* for the best way to handle this. Because this is a highly personal matter, you will have to take part in choosing the solution. What do you think?' [Situation clarification].

Client: [Somewhat disappointed, but understandingly] Well, perhaps my request is a little too simple, but you must have had problems like this before and that's why I thought somebody like you must know what to do . . . .

4 *Helper:* Yes, it is true that I have seen similar problems before, but sometimes they only look the same at first sight; your situation is different from that of other people and the way in which they handle it does not necessarily have to be your way. I therefore propose that we will together look at what you have told me and see what it means to you and what solutions you may have thought of yourself. Shall we look at these things more precisely? [Situation clarification; explanation and concreteness].

Client: Well, all right, I suppose so . . . .

In the first instance (reaction 1) the helper responds to the request for a solution with a paraphrase of that request ('You are wondering how to go on. . .'). In reaction 2 the helper begins with a reflection (the most important message sent by the client is her feeling of desperation), combined once more with an explicit paraphrase: 'and therefore you ask me: What in the world should I do?' By means of this answer the helper is checking whether he has understood the question correctly. In reaction 3 we have a situation clarification: the helper explains that he cannot just come up with an answer right away, because he lacks certain information and would prefer to work according to the cooperation model. The client demurs a little and appeals once more to the helper's expertise: 'you must have had problems like this before . . .' In reaction 4 the helper confirms that he has talked with people with comparable problems (if this is not the case, he should say so), but he differentiates the situation by saying: 'your situation is different . . .' and the way in which this client wants to handle it is something she should find out for herself. The helper explains that this is his view and concludes with a proposal: to summarize what has been discussed and search together for possible ways of dealing with the situation. The initiative and responsibility for choosing a certain course of action has thus been laid squarely on the client's shoulders. She agrees, though hesitatingly. However, it is clear again now that ready solutions will not be offered by the helper. The role of the client in looking for solutions has been restored: her role is not a passive, dependent one, but an actively responsible one.

Example 3

The client wants a more personal ('ordinary') relationship with the helper. Situation clarification here means discussing the fact that the helper is well aware of this intention of the client, as well as being quite clear about the extent to which (s)he is willing to meet this expectation.

Client: Now that we've met a few times, I'm starting to dislike the fact that all the talking is about me.

1 *Helper* [Woman]: You would actually like me to tell a little about myself as well [makes the implicit explicit].

Client: Yes, indeed, and I would also like to meet you somewhere else than just this consulting room.

2 *Helper:* Hm, hm . . . [ponders] Well, I am glad to see you like me, but still I do not want to give our relationship the form of an ordinary friendship. Our conversations are aimed at finding a solution for your problems. I want to work very hard on that, but that's as far as I want to go. This doesn't mean that I don't want to talk about myself, but I would rather do that when it links up with your problem. Can you accept that? [Situation clarification].

Client: [Looks disappointed] Yes, OK, perhaps it was a silly question . . . .

3 *Helper:* No, I don't think it was a silly question but you are a little disappointed in my answer, isn't that so? [Reflection of feeling].

Client: Well, to be honest, yes, I am.

4 *Helper*: I can understand that. Perhaps I'd better explain why I do not want that. You see, I look at it this way: when you treat each other as friends, there are interests on both sides, and so it is two-way. And that is not so in this relationship, which is one way. You have come with a request for help and I try to do my work by helping you as best I can. I can only do that in this kind of relationship and that is why I do not want a relationship apart from this one.

In this example we see the following. After the first situation clarification (reaction 2) the client reacts with some disappointment. The helper then responds understandingly with a reflection (reaction 3). This is important, because the things she says are a form of bad news, and the way to deal with bad news is to enable the client to come to terms with it by bringing it out into the open. Only after the first emotions have been processed by the client, can the cooperation continue. We also see in this example that the helper is willing to meet one of the client's wishes: to talk more about herself (reaction 2), but only when that is functional (see also p. 153, Examples of one's own). The other wish, a relation outside the professional one, is not fulfilled. In this decision both professional (mixing of roles) and personal considerations (no time, possibly no inclination) play a part (reactions 2 and 4). On pp. 83–5 the differences between a friendly relation and the professional relation have already been discussed. The example above also shows that clarification is not always pleasant. Still, this clarification is preferable to an unclear situation, in which the client – after a long wait – finally finds out by implication that the helper 'does not want a relationship apart from this (professional) one'.

In the examples described above we see that the helper takes the initiative in discussing that which is about to happen (example 1) or is happening (examples 2 and 3). When the helper fails to do so, all kinds of implicit expectations may be raised which can confuse the issue. Certain matters are kept 'under the table', with the result – as can be seen in examples 2 and 3 – that the client believes that in due course the helper will actually come up with a solution or will meet the advances of the client. There are many such situations in which uncertainties or implied expectations play a part. For instance:

- A situation in which the client finds it very hard to talk about problems.
- A situation in which the client jumps from one subject to another.
- A dialogue that goes round and round in circles and never seems to get anywhere.

For all such cases the general principle is clear: to move away from the discussion in progress (first level) and initiate meta-conversation (second level). We have developed examples of discussions on videocassette which deal with this kind of awkward situation. The title is: 'Pitfalls in the Counselling Process' (see Appendix 1).

Thinking aloud

In this book we advocate that the counsellor should be as open, clear, and straightforward as possible. This approach can best be expressed by the helper not leaving the client in the dark about his (the helper's) thoughts, but by frankly expressing them in words. By this we mean that the helper should not only tell the client about his conclusions, but also about the thoughts and considerations leading up to them.

Despite an arsenal of skills for clarifying and keeping the conversation going, there will sometimes be moments when the helper does not know exactly what to do next. To reveal his thoughts, even then, about being stuck at such a time serves several purposes.

First, the client gets to know what is on the helper's mind. This reduces his anxiety. When the helper is silent for some time without telling the client what he is thinking about, the latter may start to worry: 'What is he thinking about now? Is there really something wrong with me and is that why he is thinking so hard?' In other words, by expressing his thoughts the helper becomes more 'ordinary'.

The second function of thinking aloud is that the helper does not get stumped himself. A helper does get stuck sometimes. His saying that he now has to think for a while has a liberating effect. Moreover, it also suits the cooperation model because the client is offered an opportunity to give a response and a follow-up to this remark. Here is an example to demonstrate this:

Helper: [After a pause] At this moment *I'm thinking* about how we should go on.
Client: Yes, I am also wondering if I have really told you everything that is important.
Helper: Hm, hm [Minimal encouragement].
Client: I can't think of anything else at the moment.
Helper: OK, let's see, so far you have told me . . . [Gives a summary].

Also when asking questions, particularly questions from the helper's own frame of reference, the thinking aloud contributes to openness. The client finds out about the origin of the question. For example:

Helper: I was just thinking that I really know very little about your daily life situation. Can you tell me something more about that?

By introducing questions in this way the conversation will progress more easily and openly.

Third, we would like to point to the model function of the helper. For him to get acquainted with the client's frame of reference (his way of processing information) it is necessary for the client to 'think aloud'. When the helper also does this, the chance of the client following his example increases.

In the fourth place this behaviour advances joint cooperation; by thinking together and doing so aloud helper and client have a greater chance of finding a joint solution.

In daily life we often refrain from 'thinking aloud', especially when we feel insecure. We often ask questions from our own frame of reference without being clear about the background to these questions. In counselling we have to make a greater effort. We must be aware of the origin of our remarks and questions.

In order to train this skill systematically, Kagan (1975) has developed the so-called Interpersonal Process Recall method, in which students are trained systematically by observing themselves on video after an interview with a client. They get feedback step by step from a supervisor and from the client, and they themselves also consider which unspoken thoughts gave rise to their responses.

What is the difference between 'situation clarification' and 'thinking aloud'? First we should mention that these concepts partially overlap. However, we speak of 'situation clarification' only in the case of *obscurity or differences in mutual expectations or in the relationship itself*. There is no question of such obscurity with 'thinking aloud', for example when the helper explains the background to a certain question before posing that question. In situations where the helper feels faintly uneasy, for instance when something does not seem right in the client's story or he has the feeling that there is 'something' unclear without being able to put his finger on the exact reason, we get a combination of 'situation clarification' and 'thinking aloud'.

Helper: I was just thinking that something has been puzzling me for a while. I don't know exactly what it is, but it has something to do with what you just said . . . .

In this way, very clear to the client, the helper can try to clarify his own thought processes. When he fails to do so, the thought of something not being clear to him will remain. This detracts from the attention he needs for his client. Moreover, the client may feel that something is wrong without knowing what it is, which is also not helpful in counselling. The helper also often thinks aloud during the process of goal-evaluation; see the example on p. 123.

Should the helper now express all his thoughts aloud? Certainly not! A distinction should be made between thoughts which advance the progress of the interview and those that are unlikely to do so. Here, too, there must be a certain 'selectivity'.

Ending the counselling interview

We make a distinction between finishing the first interview, finishing subsequent interviews, and the ending of the entire contact. In this section we will deal with the first two stages jointly. In Chapter 8 the ending of the contact will be discussed.

Since time is usually limited, it is generally advisable to announce at the beginning of the interview the time available for it. In this way the duration of the interview is clear to the client, for example three-quarters of an hour, or one hour. The helper should also watch the time. This means that he must decide whether the goals set can be realized within the time limit. When time is nearly up, the helper can refer to this. For instance: 'I see that we have about five minutes left', after which he gives a summary: 'Perhaps it is a good idea to look back now at what we have discussed.' After this summary he can discuss with the client how to continue. Benjamin (1969) indicates that the helper can also ask the client to summarize what has been discussed. This has the advantage that the client is urged himself to bring some structure into the subjects under discussion.

Another possible way of ending is to conduct a meta-conversation about how the client has experienced the interview. This action is to be recommended particularly with the initial interview, since clients at the beginning are often fairly ignorant about the course of such an interview and enjoy the opportunity to say what they thought about it. For example:

Helper: We have now come nearly to the end of this first interview. Now we agreed at the beginning that our first goal would be to clarify your problems and put them in a certain order. We then discussed that . . . . [Summary]. What I wonder in general is: What did you think of this first interview?

Client: Well, eh . . . looking back I can say it wasn't so bad, for I really was a bit tense, you know. . . .

Helper: You thought it would be difficult to talk about your problems just like that with someone you didn't know. . . .

Client: That's right. After all, you don't know who you will be facing. . . .

Helper: That's true. So, you're saying it wasn't so bad after all?

Client: No, that's right.

Helper: Well, I'm glad to hear it. Another question I would like to ask you is: have we reached our goal? What do you think?

Client: Well, yes, partly, but a lot of things still aren't yet clear to me; there are other things involved as well. I don't know what I should do now.

Helper: Yes, if I understand you correctly, we are not there yet, as far as our first goal is concerned. Perhaps we should talk about that next time. You also say that you do not yet know what you should do; I don't know that myself as yet, but our goal was not to discuss everything in one session. That, too, can be discussed next time. That is to say, we can then see if we can come to a point where certain steps can be taken. Do you agree with that? Shall we try to make an appointment for next time?

Apart from the fact that talking together about the client's experience with the interview is a good way to end, it also has another function: the client becomes more confident, because he sees that *together* with the helper he can talk *about* the talk they have just had.

This strategy can also be used in the second and subsequent interviews, but we advise against concluding every interview in this way. Meta-conversation is not always functional. When it is done every time, a certain saturation point may set in. The client starts to think: 'Oh, yes, this is where we start talking about how our talk was.' Therefore it is better to *agree* that with certain intervals (for instance every fourth talk) the discussion will end with an evaluation.

Ending an interview is particularly hard when the client – often after a difficult beginning – is still in the middle of his (problematical) story. It then seems very discourteous or even inhumane to say: 'Time is up.' All the same, it is important to keep to the agreed time, even if in practice an interview will occasionally continue beyond that. But there is a risk that the client – in spite of the time limit – starts to expect that he can go on. Moreover, we sometimes see that a client tends to put off a discussion of the really important issues. Once such a pattern of expectation is formed, it becomes more and more difficult to change it. Also it depends on the time available to the helper whether there is a possibility for continuing the interview beyond the allotted time. And when the client regularly forgets the time, it is probably a good idea to discuss this pattern with him (situation clarification). For example:

Helper: I am struck by the fact that we keep running out of time. I think the reason is that we only start talking 'for real' about the things important to you after half an hour. Perhaps you find it hard to begin?

Client: Yes, I always need some time at the beginning to get going. First I always have to get used to it here. . . .

Helper: Yes, I can imagine; still, we will have to agree that in future we will try to discuss your real problems a little sooner, for it is not very satisfactory to always have to break off talking at an important point. But I really don't have any more time than this half hour. . . .

Client: OK, I'll see what I can do.

A final example of a situation where it is difficult to bring the interview to a close is when the client at the last moment brings up a major problem. Bierkens (1976) calls this the 'doorhandle phenomenon'. Obviously the client is so burdened with this problem that he only dares to talk about it when he is leaving. What should be done? Our advice is to discuss it very briefly. And, when the helper is really very short of time, a new appointment will have to be made.

The basic skills discussed here all contribute to the realization of the first general goal: problem clarification. However, their use need not be restricted to this first stage, on the contrary, they can be usefully applied in all three stages of the helping model.

In the next chapter we will discuss a number of skills important to the second stage of the counselling process. This concerns skills needed for the second goal: gaining new insights into the problem.

Chapter seven

Gaining new insights

Introduction

After the first, problem clarification stage, the goal of the second stage is to help the client get more insights into his problems. Client and helper work together to develop a different and more detailed picture of the problems so that the client is able to see a way forward.

The method used by the helper to achieve this goal is different from that used in the problem clarification stage. The method then was to stay close to the client's frame of reference, by putting himself in the client's position, by listening, reflecting, and summarizing. He now adopts a more active approach. He finds connections and gives more of his own views on the problems, though he continues to keep in touch with the client's frame of reference. In this way the client may get a different perspective on his problems, which in turn can lead to his dealing with his problems differently.

The task of the helper in this second stage is not easy. The skills the helper uses in the first stage are similar in many ways to the skills we all use as listeners in ordinary conversation with friends. The skills used in the second stage, however, are different. Suppose for example, a friend says he can't understand why his teenage children lead such unhealthy lives. Suppose you think, however: 'It's obvious to me that you set a bad example because you smoke, drink and eat too much.' In such a situation people have to be quite brave to really say what they think. Usually these things will be left unsaid, with the rationalization: 'Well, it's none of my business, it's not my place to play the schoolmaster, and we all have our faults.' But in counselling the situation is different. Someone approaches a counsellor with a problem and his task is not just to keep on good terms. When he has insights about the client which may not be pleasant to hear, it is often useful to inform the client of these insights. They can be valuable aids in solving the problems, precisely because others avoid mentioning them.

The question now is, first, how does the helper get these insights and second, how does he transmit them to the client in an acceptable and constructive manner?

Making insightful connections

In Chapters 3 and 4 we have explained which theories we use and recommend to help with the process of getting a clearer insight into the client's problems. The first criterion for the choice of theories was that they should facilitate the cooperation model. A second criterion was that these theories could be explained to 'ordinary' people. Finally we wanted theories which would help us achieve the goals of each stage of counselling. As a result of these criteria, we chose a client-centred approach for the first stage of problem clarification, and a combination of this client-centred approach with Wexler's cognitive approach and Bandura's social learning theory for the second ('gaining new insights') and the third stage ('strategies for treatment').

Other valuable sources of ideas that the helper should draw upon include his own 'view-of-the-world' (or frame of reference) acquired in the course of his own life experiences as well as other general psychological views. He should also realize that human behaviour is made up of a multitude of components, including biological and social factors. These issues were discussed in Chapter 4.

It will be clear that the helper will have many things going through his mind when he is talking to his client. During the interview all kinds of thoughts will arise concerning the connections and causes of the client's behaviour. The question is: what does the helper do with his thoughts? Before answering the question concerning the aspect of *skill*, the concept of *interpretation* should first be considered more closely.

Interpretation

According to the dictionary, 'to interpret' means 'to explain'. The verb 'to explain' contains the adjective 'plain', meaning clear. 'To interpret' therefore means 'to make clear'. To 'make clear' also implies that certain data, facts, and feelings are made understandable. They acquire a meaning in a larger context. This brings us back to the main topic of Chapter 3 in which we discussed the importance for a person to get a certain grasp or overall understanding of his world, to help him bring a certain order into his life. Interpreting in this sense is vitally important for everyone, although fortunately we do not always think about it consciously.

Following the same theme, Levy (1963) gives the following definition of interpretation: 'this is . . . what the psychological interpretation of content consists of: a redefining or restructuring of the situation through the presentation of an alternate description of some behavioral data' (Levy 1963: 5). In other words, a psychological interpretation is a different way of describing or ordering the original data. The objective is to gain new insights.

Of course it is not only helpers who interpret; everybody does it, practically all the time: 'Man is continously striving to make sense out of his experience, to impose structure, to anticipate events. . . . For this purpose he develops highly elaborate systems of coding events and hypotheses regarding the various contingencies in his experience' (Levy 1963: 10). When seen like this, man is continually interpreting. Hence Levy distinguishes between this general ubiquitous interpreting and the psychological variety that we need in helping. By the latter is meant: to interpret from a certain frame of reference or viewpoint. Since there are different personality theories (frames of reference), the kinds of interpretation will also differ. And given this variety of theories, there is no single theory which is the best *per se*. None of the personality theoretical frames of reference can pretend to be the only true one:

> interpretation is not a search for the true meaning of the event.
> Every event is subject to a vast range of interpretations. In
> psychological interpretation we apply that particular
> construction which we believe will best suit our purposes and
> which is consistent with the theoretical frame of reference we
> bring to the situation.
>
> (Levy 1963: 10)

Thus psychological interpretation means that the helper tries to place the information the client gives him into the framework of a psychological theory. Levy conceptualizes interpretations as being on a continuum. On the one side of this continuum are the interpretations which are very *closely associated with the client's frame of reference*. Things that have not yet clearly been expressed by him, are made explicit by the helper. Rogers spoke in this connection of 'what is vaguely known to the client' (see p. 29). On the other side of the continuum are interpretations in which there is a far greater distance between the things said by the helper and those that the client is aware of. We may speak here of surprising insights which the client had not thought of before. Therefore these insights lie *outside the frame of reference* of the client.

Interpretation as a skill

The question dealt with in this section is: What does the helper *do* with his interpretations? We should be aware that the helper is interpreting right from the start of the interview, even when he is only listening. He needs this interpretation to be able to understand the client. In other words, in order for him to understand the client's words and phrases they must be ordered in the helper's cognitive system.

When to interpret?

It is clear, then, that the helper does not start to interpret only when the interview has been going on for some time. During the first phase of problem clarification the 'skill' consists mainly of the helper keeping these interpretations to himself. The helper as confidant and also largely as detective will have some (preliminary) interpretations, but will keep quiet about them. Why is this necessary?

In the first place it is necessary because hasty interpretations are often wrong. The parts of the story told by the client can be seen as pieces of a jigsaw puzzle. When the helper has been presented with only a few unconnected pieces, an interpretation, a (re)ordering of what has been said, is premature. If we keep the idea of the jigsaw puzzle in mind, we also see that the risk of faulty interpretation is greater at the beginning: a 'green' piece of the puzzle is seen as part of a meadow whereas actually it belongs to a threatening thunderstorm. At the start, it wasn't known that the puzzle also contained a thunderstorm.

The second reason for being cautious about early interpretations is because we want the client to make his own re-interpretations and thus find new ways to solve his problem. To put one's problems and their background into words in a calm and trusting atmosphere can assist this process. The chance that insights will take root is greater when discovered by oneself than when discovered by others. Apart from this it enhances the client's self-confidence when he finds a solution himself. Therefore the helper has to wait, even when (and especially when) he is bursting to give an ingenious interpretation, and make such an expert impression!

Third, the helper should not be too hasty with his interpretation because the relation with his client may not yet be on such a firm footing that the latter is yet willing or able to accept new insights. New views cause a (temporary) disturbance in the client's existing 'order', leading to feelings of unrest, surprise, confusion, etc. He is unable to incorporate a new angle on his problem right away. For him to be able to handle these negative feelings, the client has to be confident that the helper will support him. This confidence is possible only with a calm, open start to the interview.

These points emphasize once again the main theme of the good interviewing model, as expressed particularly in the role of the counsellor: in his interpretations he gradually moves from those close to the client's frame of reference to interpretations some distance away from that.

Now we invite you, the reader, to do a small exercise. We will give an example of a fragment of an interview to illustrate the process of interpretation. Then we suggest (1) that you consider after each statement made by the client which thoughts/interpretations come to mind (and to distinguish between thoughts/interpretations based on your own experiences, and those resulting from the personality theories discussed in Chapters 3 and 4). Finally, (2) you can decide what your response as helper would be.

Client: [At the beginning of the first interview] I'm always so busy these days. It takes me such a long time to keep the house clean. . . .
    (1) Your thought/interpretation: . . .
    (2) Your response to the client: . . .

The reader who recalls the discussion about the ideal-image in Chapter 4 may now already be thinking of a person with a perfectionistic ideal-image. (This thought will only come to mind when one is

familiar with this concept. Without that familiarity, one merely notices in oneself a fairly neutral response, such as: 'Well, that does not
tell me very much yet.')

The helper reacting from the interpretation, 'Ah, a perfectionistic
ideal-image!' may now respond: 'Does that occur often, that you
have a strong feeling that you have to do things extremely well?'

Client: Well, no, it's just that the house keeps getting so dirty.
  (1) Your thought/interpretation: . . .
  (2) Your response to the client: . . .

Here the helper may say (paraphrasing, but still keeping to his
interpretation): 'Aha, so the things you really feel compelled to do
are all connected with keeping the house clean.'

Client: [slightly irritated] Yes, but it really is dirty all the time, the
    children make a mess, my husband leaves everything lying around
    and we live near a factory which pollutes the entire neighbour-
    hood.
    (1) Your thought/interpretation: . . .
    (2) Your response to the client: . . .

It will be clear from this example that the helper is immediately
off on the wrong track. The 'cleaning compulsion' proves to be related to other factors. The closed questions intended to check
whether he is right in his interpretation that the client is probably
the victim of a perfectionistic ideal-image, lead to irritation on her
part.

The reader and helper who have not thought at all of a 'perfectionistic ideal-image' and would therefore have had a fairly neutral
opinion on the matter, would have reacted differently and more
openly, for instance with: 'Can you tell me a little more about this?'
In that case the client, without feeling that she is now pigeon-holed
in a diagnostic category, might have elaborated on that statement.

A more open question might also have been the response of a
helper who did think of the 'ideal-image' by way of the following
train of thought:

I find that I am thinking this client has a perfectionistic ideal
image; that is a tentative interpretation, but it is still too early to
say this out loud; so I will keep this thought in the back of my
mind for the time being; it is better first to relate to the client

and then see if I had the right idea or not.

Expertise means knowing not only what to do, but also what not to do, plus a willingness to adapt one's impressions and interpretations to new information from the client.

How to interpret?

In the above example it was clear that we should guard against presenting our interpretations at an early stage. However, even when we believe that the right moment has come to discuss our interpretation with the client, we should still bear several things in mind.

Interpretations are nearly always assumptions about a possible explanation of events. This means that an interpretation should always be presented to the client in a tentative tone. The helper should be careful that his views are not taken as the final truth by the client, especially in situations where the client is greatly in awe of the helper as the expert. The client may appear to accept the interpretation but not really absorb it as a belief of his own. The helper should be very alert to see whether his interpretation is really accepted or not. An overly quick response such as: 'Yes, yes, I suppose that's right' from a client who then immediately goes on talking, should make the helper suspicious and make him wonder whether the client is really helped by this interpretation. In tone the interpretation must express a joint search between the client and the helper as the 'detective' and also as the 'teacher' who gives his explanations but is not absolutely sure that they are right.

Another significant point concerns the choice of words in the interpretation. When the helper observes that a certain psychological theory seems to fit the facts and explain the problem, he should not offer that explanation in abstract theoretical terms, but in everyday language familiar to the client. The following illustrates a wrong and right way of doing this:

Helper 1: According to Bandura's social learning theory it often happens that people are aware of the effectiveness of a certain action, in your case talking with your boyfriend, but that they do not consider themselves capable of bringing such an action to a successful end.

Helper 2: I can see you are still doubtful; perhaps you are thinking: I really should talk to my boyfriend, but I can't yet see myself actually doing it.

In both cases the helper makes use of the same theory in his interpretation. In both cases he is on the right track and chooses the right moment. But the first interpretation is likely to be experienced as cool and detached and perhaps incomprehensible and hence as disagreeable by the client, for the helper chooses language suitable for a theoretical treatise. Theories are intended for making relatively general statements. By talking in this way to his client, he is classifying her as one of a certain group, so that her problem loses its individual significance. She becomes an object to be studied and explained. The helper has forgotten one step. He ought to realize that he is cooperating with a fellow human being who is an individual in her own right.

The process of putting interpretations into words is not only difficult when it concerns psychological interpretations based on theoretical insights. Problems also occur where the helper's own interpretations are concerned. Sometimes the helper feels like saying, 'Now look, it is quite obvious that you have to talk to that man of yours, and give him a piece of your mind!' This impulse should be translated in such a way that the client will not feel like a coward for not daring to take the most obvious measures herself. This does not imply that the helper should always be cautious with his client, but that he should take the situation and the client's use of language into account.

Giving information

In the previous section we discussed how the helper should only use his theoretical knowledge in a way that suits the client. However, it is not necessarily always a bad idea to talk to the client in a more scholarly manner about the theories and views held by the helper relating to the client's problems. We have already mentioned that we prefer theories that are simple enough to explain to a client. In Chapter 5 we also said that there are advantages in explaining one's way of working to the client. Our aim was to give the helper – in his role as teacher – an opportunity to keep the client as fully informed as possible. When the helper suspects his client of holding unconstructive views, it may be useful to teach him a game in psychology. For example:

Helper: I keep hearing you say, 'I'm so slow in everything I do' or 'I'm always such a coward', as if that's the way you are all the time and in all situations. But in psychology we have found that people often think that they have these fixed attributes, but when you look at how they actually behave in different situations they act in very different ways. Therefore I would like to check with you more precisely if maybe there are situations where you are not so slow or are not a coward.

Other objective information, for example, from questionnaires and tests, can also be used to help the client gain greater knowledge and insights during this second stage of counselling. But the helper should ensure that the meaningfulness of such tests is clearly understood by the client.

Differentiating skills

In this section we will describe a number of clearly distinguishable skills that can be viewed as operationalizations of interpretation. We will first give an overview of these differentiating skills.

Overview of differentiating skills

- Advanced accurate empathy.
- Confrontation.
- Positive relabelling.
- Examples of one's own.
- Directness.

Advanced accurate empathy

The concept of 'advanced accurate empathy' should be seen against the background of basic empathy, discussed in the previous chapter, consisting of the skills of paraphrasing of content, reflection of feeling, and summarizing. We refer now to the distinction mentioned before that Levy makes between interpretations close to the client's frame of reference and those that are some distance away from it, but which none the less give a sharper or more constructive view of the problem. Advanced accurate empathy belongs to the latter group.

With this skill the helper not only shows understanding by accurately reflecting the feelings expressed by the client, for example, but also by bringing out the half-hidden emotional tone in the client's story. He listens keenly to what is said between the lines, and attends closely to the client's non-verbal behaviour. It is then a matter of translating these latent ideas and feelings of the client into words. Sometimes these concern subjects which the client hardly dares to touch upon or matters that he has trouble facing: 'bad' sides of himself, embarrassing connections between certain events. Let us try to put in concrete terms what we mean by 'to listen keenly'.

First, while listening to the client the helper can use the context of the story, as well as what he knows from earlier conversations with the client. To continue with the metaphor used before, he can make a connection between several pieces of the jigsaw puzzle.

In the second place the tone in which the client speaks and his whole manner of expressing himself also contain valuable information. When giving such information back to the client the helper is one step ahead of the client as it were; this gives the client some insight into things not immediately visible to him before. For example:

Client: [Looking anxious and moving about on his chair] Well, my girlfriend keeps on saying I do everything wrong, and, well, I just don't know what to do any more.

An empathizing helper might respond with:

You are beginning to doubt yourself because you never do anything right in her eyes.

A more advanced and differentiated empathic response goes beyond that. For example:

You are beginning to have doubts because you never do things right in your girlfriend's eyes, but I also hear an anxious note there, in the sense of: I hope she will not leave me?

In this last example we see the helper reproducing not one but two still latent thoughts as well as the accompanying emotions. He thereby shows a greater understanding than in the first example, while the client is also induced to a further exploration of his feelings.

A third way to make use of advanced accurate empathy is to make connections between several parts of the client's story. For example:
Helper: You told me that you've been drinking quite a lot lately and that your marriage is not running smoothly at the moment. It looks as if there is a connection between the two . . . what do you think about that?

The client had mentioned these two problems separately, without seeing a connection himself. This connection may not exist at all, and the helper should therefore present his interpretations in a tentative way. Making connections is also important because it gives the client something to hold on to, particularly in the case of undefined emotions, such as vague fears or listlessness, where the client is completely at a loss about the origin of these feelings. However, we should point out that in these cases the chance of influencing the client is greatest, in that there is a risk that the client concurs with connections which in reality do not exist. An interesting point here is the question of when connections 'really' exist. With personal problems this is often very hard to say. Connections are 'real' when someone is convinced that they exist.

A fourth way to express advanced accurate empathy can be found in the skill of 'summarizing', discussed in the previous chapter. Advanced accurate empathy here means that the helper knows how to place the main points in a certain sequence. A concrete suggestion to promote this is given by Egan (1975). In his opinion the use of 'newsprint' is advisable. This means that an inventory is made on a blackboard or on paper of the main problematical points, as well as of the resources available to the client:

> Newsprint summaries can be used to list the client's salient
> feelings, experiences, and behaviors, his newly acquired
> understandings of himself and their concomitant demand for
> action, and the working out of the action programs themselves
> in terms of both planning and execution, successes and failures.
> The helper can let the client know that he, too, may use the
> newsprint, or he can teach him how to do so. This is another
> way the helpee can become more of an agent in the helping
> process.
>
> (Egan 1975: 143)

The use of advanced accurate empathy is one of the ways in which to arrive at the second stage: to order the information given by the client in such a way that he gets a broader, more differentiated view of his problems.

Confrontation

The skill of confrontation is a more pronounced form of advanced accurate empathy. The helper uses interpretations that are quite distant from the client's frame of reference.

In ordinary usage, to confront means to compare, to place opposite each other. The concept also often implies roughness, hostility, for example, to confront a criminal with his victim in order to make him confess. To be confronted with reality means to come up against the hard facts. In counselling, to confront means that the helper gives a response to the client's views about himself or his world that is significantly different from that of the client. In that sense there is indeed some roughness involved here. For usually one of the characteristics of confrontation is that it has an 'unmasking' effect (Egan 1975). Everyone (occasionally) presents himself as 'better' than he really is, because he believes this to be the 'best' he can do. We put on a mask in order to protect ourselves, our vulnerability. A mask also makes us feel freer. During carnivals people put on masks so that they can behave in a silly way without being recognized. Therefore it is, understandably, quite unfair and against the rules of the game to pull off somebody's mask. How, then, can a figurative unmasking be reconciled with any form of helping, which after all is meant to leave people their dignity and even to enhance that dignity?

Let us first state that we are not so moralistic as to advocate that everyone should always be 'himself' and should live without a mask. In the first place this is difficult, while furthermore it would mean a denial of an important and positive means of protection in many difficult situations.

All the same, it can happen that someone gets stuck with the image he has of himself and/or gives of himself to the outside world. All the skills discussed are intended to contribute to a solution in a problematical situation. The objective of confrontation is also to present the client with a different vision of himself or his environment, in order to get the problematical situation moving again.

We also ought to realize that there is a difference between the content of the confrontation and our way of presenting it. In ordinary behaviour people are only inclined to confrontation when they 'are going to tell somebody the truth'; they get themselves worked up by saying, 'He's not going to like this.' More or less consciously the thought is, 'If I don't tell him off very firmly, he is certainly not going to agree.' In short, the aggressive, reproachful, mocking, or perhaps desperate tone colours the confrontation. All this does not fit in very well with our form of helping. It is therefore essential that a confrontation is presented in a quiet, businesslike, suggestive, and especially accepting tone of voice to the client.

Helper: Now you have told me a lot about the various jobs you have held and that it was always the boss who caused the problems. In this job, too, you are likely to get fired because the boss is so difficult. But I never hear you talk about your share in these problems; it is always only the other person . . . ?

A 'tone' is hard to express in written words, but we hope to have indicated that in the example there is both the confrontation and the possibility for the client to 'save face', as well as a chance that the helper is wrong, but particularly that the (onesided) view of the client is also acceptable. There are quite a few arguments in favour of this kind of confrontation.

In the first place we must bear in mind that everyone has his own way of thinking about himself and others, in order to defend his respect for himself and others. When that way of thinking is suddenly damaged by confrontation, our reaction is one of fright. Either the client is not aware of this unrealistic image of himself and has to adjust to the new one, or he tries to paint too good a picture of himself. However, a calm and accepting attitude by the helper can make it possible for the client to assess the confrontation at face value. The client finds that the helper keeps on accepting him, that he acts normally and does not accuse him. 'Maybe it's not so bad to admit to him and to myself that I am sometimes a difficult person.' Such a revolution in the client's thinking and doing is at the heart of the counselling process. To dare to look at one's own shortcomings, to dare to confess to them, is often a major breakthrough and the startingpoint for constructive changes.

The suggestive tone in a confrontation is intended to make it easier for the client to dispute the confrontation. Often in the professional literature (Egan 1982; Berenson and Mitchell 1976) the assumption is that the helper is right in his surmise and that the client has not (yet) arrived at the insight of the helper. In our view this standpoint is too pretentious. A helper is human too, and also has his blind spots, which means that he may be totally wrong in his confrontation. It is good when a helper exercises some caution with regard to his being right.

It may also be a good idea for a client, even when the helper has guessed correctly in his confrontation, not to accept it right away. After all, we humans know very little about each other, about our complex and tangled inner lives. A confrontation may be so overwhelming that the client is not up to it, not even with an accepting helper nearby. In such cases the client probably acts in his best interest in denying this insight, consciously or unconsciously, however irrational the helper finds this.

The use of a calm and businesslike tone in a confrontation helps to give the client time. This is necessary because considering and processing a confrontation does take time. A new ordering of information is about to take place. Perhaps the processing takes so much time that at first the client cannot accept the confrontation. We all experience the tendency to deny a confrontation, but perhaps, lying in bed at night, we start thinking, 'Well, there may be something in it after all.' When the client does not immediately concur with the confrontation it does not mean that he does not do anything with it. What he does is often very hard to find out. At least it is a nice thought for the helper and will keep him going!

It is clear that the use of confrontation depends very much on the helper's sense of responsibility. It goes without saying that he should not go on cramming a confrontation down his client's throat when the latter does not accept it. And the helper should not even embark on a confrontation if he suspects that his alternative view of a problem is not going to help the client. To confront someone with his inability to deal with people, without being capable of improving this inability, only makes a client more unhappy, for which the helper is to blame. Research has shown that effective helpers use confrontations more sparingly than bad helpers, measured by a complete judgement of their performance (Berenson and Mitchell 1976).

Confronting is a complex skill; the essence lies in the shock effect for the client. However, other skills described by us also contain this. A concise summary may also yield connections that can shock. A request for concretization may have a sobering effect:

Client: I have really tried everything to stop smoking!
Helper: What exactly have you tried?
Client: Well, uh. . . .

One remaining question concerns the discrepancies with which the helper confronts the client. Different authors here offer different classifications (Egan 1982; Nelson-Jones 1982). There are, for instance, discrepancies between verbally and non-verbally expressed feelings.

Client: [Looking annoyed] Well, I really am not angry with that man at all.

Helper: The way in which you say that makes me suspect that you are [or] Well, you sound rather annoyed.

Nelson-Jones describes a number of possible areas of discrepancy, such as:

- Utterances in and behaviour outside counselling:

You say that you don't care what your friends think of you, but you also say that you are always so tense when you are with them?

- Utterances in and intentions outside counselling:

You have already indicated several times that you want to spend more time with your children, but it does not seem to work out that way?

- Attribution of responsibility and behaviour:

You believe that you are completely responsible for your own actions, yet I keep hearing you blaming your boyfriend, that he is the cause of your bad relationship?

In referring to further points on confrontation, Egan mentions all manners of tricks, games, and vaguenesses by which people seek to misrepresent reality or their own functioning, to present themselves as better or different, to avoid situations, or just not talk about 'awkward' subjects. Difficult decisions in life are often postponed. In such situations the helper, before confronting the client, should show some understanding for his difficulties. For example:

Helper: I can well imagine that you are not looking forward to that talk with your mother, but what happens if you keep putting it off?

So far, confrontation has been described as a skill. The helper faces the client with his weak points or at least draws his attention to embarrassing discrepancies. Berenson and Mitchell (1976), however, point out that besides 'weakness confrontation', attention should also be paid to 'strength confrontation'. By the latter they mean that one of the tasks of the helper is to teach his client to find out about his strong points and not continue to emphasize a number of weak points. It is very necessary to stress this aspect of confrontation. Professional helpers are accustomed to paying attention to their client's problems (in other words, weak points). These they know best, for they are what they have 'studied for'. Moreover, the client must justify his presence to the helper. Hence he talks about his problems and shortcomings; together they make for a rather gloomy picture.

Berenson and Mitchell (1976) report in their research results that there are considerable differences between effective and less effective helpers, especially regarding the type of confrontation used. Poor helpers use 'weakness confrontations' fifteen times as much as good helpers, especially with more vulnerable clients. In short, helper please note: if a client is looking for a way out of his difficulties and if he wants to enhance his self-respect, attention to his strong points – of which he may himself not even be aware – is of primary importance:

Helper: You say that people don't like you, but you also mentioned that Bill has invited you to go on holiday with him?

The question now arises whether the helper should start mentioning these strong points immediately the client starts to talk about his weak ones. We believe this is not indicated, and in fact would show little understanding. Berenson and Mitchell give a useful indication which fits into our interviewing model. They suggest that confrontations should move progressively from 'weaknesses' to 'strengths', converging in an 'action confrontation' such as: 'and what are you going to do, now that we know about your strong points?' We should remind the reader that, generally speaking, confrontations of the above kind are unsuitable at the beginning of a contact. As they become more challenging, they require a stronger trusting relationship and that needs time to grow.

Positive relabelling

In connection with emphasizing the client's strong points through confrontation, we want to discuss an alternative which also aims at giving the client some positive insights.

Positive relabelling means: to apply a new, positive reconstruction to the parts of the problem originally found to be negative. The purpose of positive relabelling is to place the client's 'sick' aspects in a favourable light. This definition is important because 'positive relabelling' can easily be confused with the stressing of the 'healthy aspects'. With positive relabelling, however, an attempt is made to give a favourable meaning to the complaints and symptoms themselves: their presence in some way signifies a favourable development. Thus positive relabelling does not mean that the client is told that besides the shadowy sides of his problem there is also a sunny side.

Apart from giving a new reconstruction of the problem, a second characteristic of positive relabelling is that a positive motive is given to what is supposed to be the cause of the problem.

In order not to become too abstract, we will give a number of examples.

1 *Client:* I loathe myself for being so terribly slow. I really am disgustingly slow and lazy.
   Helper: Still, this slowness, as far as I can see, is due to the fact that you first want to think carefully about things.
2 *Client:* I don't understand why I said those nasty things to my mother; I think that was a very mean thing to do.
   Helper: At any rate, you have been frank. At least your mother now knows what you think of her.

3 Lange (1980) gives the example of a woman who believes that she is too hurried and agitated in everything she does, which would make her tense. Her helper did not agree with this explanation, and gave another interpretation:

> The pace with which you do things suits your lively personality and makes it possible for you to be interested in several things at the same time. I think you would be more tense if you went against your nature.

In all three examples we see that:

- the behaviour judged negatively by the client is placed in another context;
- it is assumed that a positive motive is at the base of the behaviour considered negatively by the client.

Functions of positive relabelling

The most important function of this skill is that the negative self-image of the client is altered. The slowness of the client in example 1 is linked to an intelligent, cautious approach to life. The saying of 'nasty things' by the client in example 2 is labelled as frankness. The agitation of the client in example 3 suits her 'lively personality'.

When the client concurs with the positive relabelling, a consequence for the counselling process may be that in a number of cases the client need not necessarily alter his or her behaviour, or at least not to the extent originally aspired to. The client from example 1 does not have to set as his goal that he should do everything more quickly, when he realizes that his pace is the result of a desirable thinking-through approach. Conversely, the client in example 3 need not do everything more slowly. Both clients, after having processed this insight, can decide that they are content with the present situation. However, there is a middle course: the client from example 1 keeps to his decision to work a little faster, but his aim is not as high as in the beginning. The client from example 3 can on the whole maintain her quick pace, but she may strive to be a little calmer in some situations. In the foregoing a second function of relabelling is demonstrated: as a result of a more differentiated look at the problems, it is easier to decide what steps should be taken to do something about them.

A third function of positive relabelling is that the helper can help to offset undesirable standards of behaviour which may be the norm in the client's social environment. Let us take one more look at the example of the 'agitated woman'. She may formerly not have found her own behaviour odd in any way: simply quick off the mark, a little hurried. The agitation only became a problem when she found herself in an environment of slower persons who began to criticize 'all that busy-busy way of doing things'. She finds herself no longer quick off the mark, but agitated!

Frequently the intolerant norms of an environment of a client with an idiosyncratic character, thoughts, or behaviour cause problems for the client:

Client: I often cry about sad things, I can't help myself there; that is why they told me I was unstable and had to see a doctor and he has referred me to you.

The client must then be told that emotionality does not mean that one is unstable *per se*, but that crying about sad situations may also be evidence of a healthy expression of one's feelings.

Generally speaking, it can be said that in society we have norms for behaviour in certain situations that do not leave enough room for everyone's own reactions. For example, a woman has suddenly lost her husband through a fatal accident. The overwhelming grief results in an absence of violent emotions, a pale countenance, while for the rest she is continually washing and cleaning. For the moment that is the only way she can keep going. The neighbourhood is surprised: 'She is not sad at all.' The questions she is asked about this also cause doubts in herself: 'Didn't I love him? I am so quiet inside; I feel nothing.'

The helper here would try to give an explanation which shows understanding for her grief as well as for her way of trying to cope with this blow, and which indicates that there are many ways to be sad. This may at least help to remove the doubt concerning her feelings for her husband. Thus the helper has an important compensating function, which he can only fulfil when he identifies with the client, dissociates himself from his own prejudices, and carefully considers the client's circumstances.

Indication for the application of positive relabelling

What are the situations or the times when the use of this skill is called for? From the above examples we can distil two general rules. To apply a positive label is desirable:

- When the client himself gives a negative explanation for his behaviour, thoughts, or feelings leading to a worsening of the problematical situation. Positive relabelling can be seen here as a correction by the helper.
- When the client cannot account for the problematical situation. 'I don't understand why I say these things' (see example 2). 'I don't understand why I feel so tense.' Usually the effect of positive relabelling here is that the client regains a hold on the incomprehensible situation.

Whenever possible, it is better that the client first thinks of possible explanations himself before being presented with a positive one by the helper. However, when the client fails to see a way out, a credible and positive motive suggested by the helper can be very supportive.

The question remains, of course, whether the client agrees with the positive alternative. This will largely depend on the credibility of the interpretation. It should be emphasized that with positive relabelling one should guard against a belittling of 'real' problems. Often it is better to face certain negative aspects of life first rather than quickly turn them into positive factors.

Examples of one's own

By 'examples of one's own' we mean that the helper shares some of his own experiences with the client and thus shows what is on his mind or has been in the past. This skill is often referred to as self-disclosure.

This skill has several functions in counselling. The first is that by talking about a comparable experience, the helper shows that what the client is going through is something shared – the helper recognizes the situation. This has the advantage of reducing the distance between them, thus raising the quality of the relationship. This is important since clients often look up to a helper.

Another function of giving 'examples of one's own' is that the fact that the helper talks about himself, increases the chance that the client will also reveal his personal views.

A third function is to help the client put into words those things that he cannot or dare not express himself. This function of the own example is particularly suitable if the relationship between counsellor and client is well-established. A client, for example, may have trouble confessing that occasionally he dislikes his friend wholeheartedly. The helper recognizes this and says, 'I also experience that sometimes, that I really hate my partner for what he does, even though I love him dearly . . . is it something like that?'

By putting such thoughts into words the helper says out loud something of which the client thinks, 'But that can't be, that thought should not even enter your mind when you care for someone.' By quietly saying this, without shame or pride, the helper shows that he also accepts his own shortcomings and more generally his tolerance for human weaknesses, thus making it easier for the client to be open about his own thoughts and feelings.

An application of this skill is indicated when the helper has the impression that the client will find it easier to talk about his experiences and feelings when he himself does so as well. It can also be a good idea to talk about oneself at the beginning of an interview. In that case this skill contributes to the goal that goes with the first stage of the contact, which is to establish a trusting relationship.

In the example we see that what the helper says about himself is closely related to the client's frame of reference. If that were not the case, the giving of an example of one's own would probably be counterproductive and would merely lead the client astray.

Another point is that the helper should guard against an artificial and frequent use of this skill. A helper who continuously claims that he recognizes the problem makes the client suspicious and may lead to a loss of credibility. A too frequent use can also result in the helper's problems being discussed more than those of the client, as is the case in the following example:

Client: Maybe I have taken on too much: my job, evening classes, I belong to two athletic clubs, and then I also have to keep up my social contacts.

Helper: Yes, I know what you're talking about. I have also had such a period, or rather: I still have it. Sometimes it really gets me down.

Client: I am sorry to hear that. What exactly do you do?

The roles are reversed when the helper starts to tell the client all about his own problems, which is certainly not the intention.

Directness

Directness implies that there is a frank discussion about what is happening in the here-and-now situation of the contact between client and helper. Hence Egan (1975) calls this skill also the 'you-me-talk', others call it 'immediacy' (Carkhuff 1969) or 'direct mutual communication' (Ivey 1971).

The first aim of directness is to promote further joint cooperation between helper and client. In this respect it is similar to 'situation clarification' (p. 124), but since we are concerned here with the second, insight-giving stage of counselling the level of understanding in the relation goes deeper. It is no longer restricted to talking about joint cooperation and expectations but also concerns the personal relationship between helper and client. For example:

Helper: I would like to discuss with you how you react when I ask you something. This seems important to me on account of your problem, which is that you find it hard to communicate. . . .

Client: Oh yes, oh yes, I often think that people. . . .

Helper: Now wait a minute! Let me finish, that's what it is all about.

Client: What do you mean?

Helper: When I ask you a question, you always answer very briefly and then you keep on talking for a long time, jumping from one subject to another. Do you recognize that happening?

Client: Yes, I do, but there are a lot of issues involved here; I mean, my parents, and what has happened in the past and now this relationship with my boss and. . . .

Helper: No, wait, there you go again. . . . I want to say something else as well. For you have – like now – a tendency to pay no attention to me at all. This is a little offputting for me, as if you think: what he says is not really important. Do you understand what I mean?

Client: Yes . . . yes.

Helper: Perhaps other people also react to you in this way, but in ordinary life people would not often say that they find something off-putting. Do you believe this may happen with other people?

In this example we see how the helper raises the matter of the client's way of saying things (skipping from one subject to another), as well as his tendency not to pay attention to the other person, in order to find out if there is a pattern here. We also see that the client, while talking about it, also shows this same behaviour.

Another goal of this skill is to give the client an idea of the consequence of his behaviour. After all, many clients complain of difficulties in their interpersonal relations. And often they are not aware themselves of the effect of their words and behaviour on others. By explicitly drawing attention to this effect, the counsellor is helping the client to learn something new. He learns to observe his own behaviour and to recognize the consequences of what he says and does. On the basis of the insight thus acquired he can decide if he wants to bring about some changes in that behaviour.

However, we have to make certain reservations. The helper is only one person and his response to the behaviour (verbal or nonverbal) of the client need not be the same as that of others, and he needs to make this clear. This form of directness also differs from what in daily life is understood by 'directness', that is to say, to express without inhibitions, possibly in an accusing tone of voice, our displeasure with the other person's behaviour.

The helper should be careful not to make very broad generalizations. The directness must be tentative in tone: does the client recognize that he evokes this sort of reaction of irritation in others? Finally, remember that directness contains a confrontation. The client may be alarmed or frightened by the discovery of patterns of behaviour in himself that he was not aware of, and this may have such a negative effect that the helper needs to use his supportive skills at this point.

Generally speaking, 'directness' is indicated in two cases. The first is when the helper himself feels uncomfortable about the progress of the interview and believes that this can be improved by speaking about these feelings and their possible cause. The second is when the helper has the idea that the client has difficulty putting certain thoughts and feelings into words. We see an example of this in the following:

Helper: I occasionally see you looking at me as if to say, yes, this man is listening to me all right, nodding and doing his best, but can he really help me . . . ?

Client: Well, now that you mention it . . . yes, I did not really have the courage to say it myself, but I do have the feeling that we are not making much progress and then I wonder, does he really know enough about it, after all, he is only human too. . . .

In the discussion following this, the fact that the helper does have sufficient knowledge of the problems should be made clear, but a more important thing has happened: the client has revealed his thoughts and feelings about the helper which hampered contact. And this in turn increases the possiblity of finding a way out – in trust.

We must strike a cautionary note here: the application of the skill 'directness' should only be used when a certain trusting relationship has been established.

Like 'examples of one's own', this skill also has a modelling function: the helper is showing by example that it is possible to discuss what is happening 'here and now'. By becoming alerted to this in counselling, the client may realize that, by using this possibility outside the counselling situation as well, he may have a better chance to improve his interpersonal functioning.

However, if the client wants to adopt this skill of the helper in normal life he should be cautioned that the nature of the relationship with his fellow human beings differs considerably from that with his helper. The client can be told that 'directness' in normal relations is useful, when its aim is to help people to get on better. For example, you are talking with someone about a certain subject and are getting annoyed because he will never let you finish what you are saying. You can then say, 'I don't like being continually interrupted; I let you finish, now you must do the same for me!' Or, even shorter: 'Let me finish what I'm saying!' But you do not afterwards return to this by saying: 'And it is also very useful for you to pay attention to this, for it will improve your relations with others!'

Directness can be seen as a combination of the skills 'examples of one's own' and 'confrontation'. On the one hand the helper talks about his own thoughts and feelings, while on the other the client is also confronted with new information relating to personal matters.

These sorts of situation are not only difficult for the client. To be direct without also expressing disapproval, annoyance, or other negative feelings is not always easy for the helper. He must find a balance between being too critical and condemning and too detached and logical in naming the subjects under discussion. Directness is a skill requiring considerable congruence on the part of the helper, as discussed in Chapter 3. When he finds himself responding impatiently to the client – who may well notice this – he should discuss this impatience or his doubts. This will also make it clear to the client exactly what is the matter. It is usually better to act like this than to say nothing, which may start the client imagining all kinds of things.

Finally, it is not only the helper who is sometimes direct. The client, too, can surprise the helper by saying, 'I have the impression that you are not listening to me today, I must say I don't like that at all.' If the client is right, the helper is better off acknowledging this: 'You're right, I am a little absentminded, I'm sorry – I will pay better attention now. OK?' When it is relevant, the helper may also mention the reason for his absentmindedness. Thus, by exploring and searching, using all kinds of skills, the helper tries to enable his client to get a better view of his problem.

Chapter eight

Strategies for treatment

Introduction

Having completed our discussion of the skills needed to help the client explore (Chapter 6) and gain insight (Chapter 7) into his problems, we turn to the skill involved in *doing* something about the problems by helping the client to change his behaviour.

Before starting on this it may be useful to summarize the various forms of 'treatment' already dealt with during the clarification and insight-gaining stages. We will then discuss a general strategy to be used in action programmes. Finally, the question of ending the contact with the client will be discussed.

Treatment

The client's own attempts

As helpers we ought to realize that a client usually has already struggled with his problem for quite a while before he comes to a counsellor. He has tried everything to solve it, with or without the help of relatives, friends, or others close to him. Every one of us has problems, large or small, that we prefer to deal with within our own resources.

It may be useful for the helper to ask himself: has the client up to now kept the problems to himself and suffered them alone or has he tried to share them? Is he trying to bring them to a satisfactory conclusion himself or has he sought the help of others in trying to get 'better' and have these others helped him?

The helper who realizes that his position is more or less halfway between the arising of a problem and its solution, will pay particular attention to the way in which the client has tried to deal with the problem himself. Gaining information on this process has considerable advantages. First, it enhances the helper's insight into the client's view of his problem and his expectations about the desired outcome. This is vital in view of unspoken differences which may exist on this point between client and helper. Second, it saves the helper some unnecessary work, because in questioning the client on his own efforts he can immediately link up with these without irritating the client with action plans he has already tried 'long ago'.

Levels of treatment

We have consistently emphasized that the ultimate goal of treatment is decided upon in close consultation with the client. In the broadest terms it is a question of helping the client to become happier without 'damaging' his social environment. A sub-goal leading up to that may be to help the client to come to grips with his own functioning and the world he lives in. In Chapters 3 and 4 we have discussed in that respect how important it is that the client is able to create some order in his world. In the creation of that 'order' we can distinguish several methods by which the client can gain 'control'. We will now have a brief look at these methods of control. We shall see that they by no means imply that treatment should always signify actions aimed directly at a change of behaviour. We will discuss three levels of 'control': naming, acceptance, and action.

Naming

For many people it is a frightening experience to find in themselves or their environment a 'phenomenon' that they cannot place or give a name to, thus making it impossible to incorporate this into their own way of thinking. In other words, people strive to 'understand' themselves and their world, and are frightened by the apparently 'incomprehensible', and have a need to name or label the phenomena.

A 45-year-old man who had always been healthy and slept like a log, suddenly finds himself waking up at night; he does not understand this sudden insomnia. The first step towards control and diminishing of the ensuing confusion is when he manages to distance himself sufficiently to observe that something is wrong. As soon as he can say to himself, 'I don't understand what is the matter with me,' he has taken the first step. So long as this distance has not been taken, there remains a sense of inner chaos which may lead to non-specific anxiety.

Barendregt (1982) describes this unnameable anxiety with the term 'it'. Clients in the initial interview talk about this: 'it' is something that there are no words for. The concept of anxiety or fear already has a name, but 'it' is different: 'it' is not a fear, you only get that when 'it' has happened. We are talking here about person-threatening experiences which Barendregt places under the heading 'depersonalization experiences'. A phobia, on the other hand, is the form in which the unnameable is given shape and content through its coupling to a phenomenon.

It is important to emphasize that the naming of 'it' contributes to the fitting-in of certain experiences in the client's ordering system – his way of thinking about the world. This leads to a greater control of this phenomenon and hence to a diminishing of anxiety.

When the man with sleeping problems has put this fear into words, and even goes on to 'discover' a reason for it (for example, he has worked too hard), he can still worry about it, but the worst is over: he has placed the phenomenon in his ordering system.

Phenomena in the outside world can also frighten us when we are unable to explain or place them. When primitive man, without knowing anything about meteorology, observed thunder and lightning, it was very frightening. When, however, he could name and explain it by seeing it as being caused by the flickering sword and thundering chariot of the god of thunder, there was already some measure of control, though it could still frighten him. Ordering and giving a meaning to events through cognitive processes lead to greater peace of mind. We are touching here upon a very interesting subject, for what we are actually saying is that people's peace of mind does not depend on the correct explanation of events and problems but on its acceptability to oneself. Thus the 'treatment' of a problem begins as soon as it is put into words. In many cases the worst is over for a client when he is able to talk about his problems.

Acceptance

A second form of control over one's own life is acceptance – a theme emphasized not only in this book, but also in cognitive behavioural therapy in general (Trower *et al.* 1988) and rational-emotive therapy in particular (Ellis 1974). The woman referred to earlier whose ideals are too high with regard to her behaviour towards her husband or the customers in her shop, sets her standards a little lower or does not mind so much when she does not do things as well as she would like to (see p. 52). She accepts her own 'shortcomings' and also the shortcomings of the other salespersons in the shop a little more easily.

The principles of acceptance can be applied in nearly all walks of life. For example, a person can get into difficulties if as he gets older he does not accept his reduced capacity for lengthy, concentrated work or his failing memory. To fight this type of phenomenon by working even harder or refusing to use a diary does not solve anything; on the contrary, it adds to the problem.

To acknowledge one's own limitations and to accept them, can help to reduce the problem. It is not a question here of only accepting one's own limitations but also those of others. To accept the undesired but unchanging behaviour of a partner can mean the end of much fighting and bitterness for both parties – and may even increase the chances of change coming about. In a broader sense it is a general principle to accept life as it is. We should actually be as amazed at everything that goes well in our own situation or in the world around us as we are aggravated and amazed at everything that is not going according to our wishes. In his memoirs Pannekoek, imprisoned during the war, writes:

> For the first time I feel a need here for philosophy, not for
> myself but for all those who have never wondered why they were
> living such a pleasant life and who are now asking wide-eyed
> about the meaning of all this misery. . . .
> (translation of Pannekoek 1982: 72)

But isn't 'acceptance' simply giving in to circumstances? Well, partly it is. We are back here with the theme of the person who gives a meaning to his own life and the events occurring around him. He can fight and protest or feel victimized throughout his life because he has not achieved his goal. But it is also possible to let go of certain demands, to acknowledge impossibilities, and to try to come to terms with one's own shortcomings. Often the result is that energy is released for more achievable goals, thus giving one better control over one's personal situation in so far as it is controllable. It is not always a sign of cowardice or weakness to accept certain problems; rather, it shows wisdom and a sense of reality. To foster this acceptance is a very powerful form of helping, particularly since in our culture we place such a high value on 'getting our own way', on 'standing on our rights', and 'realizing the ultimate goal'.

We would like to add that acceptance is only one form of the 'solving of problems' discussed here. We want to stress this because we could easily be upbraided for aiming at a lessening of a fighting spirit, of urging the individual to adapt to the existing order of respectability. Not that we find the existing Western order so bad, precisely because it leaves so much room for diversity in thinking and doing. All the same, we prefer a liberating and emancipatory form of helping, for both men and women. This means that the helper should not impose on the client his own norms, either for well-adjusted behaviour or for ideals demanding a more combative performance.

Action

A third way to achieve greater control is for the client to intervene directly and actively in a problem situation himself. The client tries to act differently from the way he did before, or tries to tackle a situation he has hitherto avoided. For instance, it is not the helper who goes to talk with the saleswoman's boss or her subordinates, but the saleswoman herself who endeavours to do something about her problem with them. The housewife heading for a nervous breakdown because her children are so demanding, will herself try to create some space for rest and for her own activities.

On the basis of insights acquired through counselling, a client may initiate such actions spontaneously. The client sees what he should or could do and undertakes the task with sufficient self-confidence and knowledge to carry out his plans. In a proper cooperative relationship the client will tell the helper about his plans and will even occasionally apply his new insights without consulting the helper. Such steps, taken on his own initiative, deserve support from the helper.

However, sometimes the client when undertaking certain activities will face disappointments, for instance when he has acted too hastily by wanting to change everything at once, or when other people react negatively to his altered behaviour. Someone who has difficulty making contact and who now has the insight that he does not have to wait for others to take the initiative but can take the initiative himself, will be disappointed when this initiative is not rewarded.

In such cases of disillusionment the advice to the helper is: sympathize with the disappointment and then look, together with the client, for other, more effective means to reach the objective, in a point we return to.

Combining levels of control

The different levels of control have so far been discussed separately. However, it is also possible that all three of them may be important for treating the same problem. The 45-year-old man from the previous example, who is afraid because he does not understand his sudden inability to sleep, may go through various phases of treatment: naming and explaining the insomnia resulting from too much work; acceptance of the necessity, also in view of his age perhaps, to take things a little more easily, to be less ambitious and keep demands from the outside world at bay; action to carry out these plans and thus to continue functioning at a healthy level – healthy, because demands and possibilities are balanced.

In the next section we will go further into the helper's strategy as coach in bringing about these changes.

Goal-directed action

The three levels of control just described will frequently culminate in some action by the client. But action alone is not enough – it needs to be directed to a goal, in other words, it needs to be part of a strategy to achieve something. In practice, after the exploration and insight stages, the time arrives when the client (together with the helper in his role as coach) has to decide which problem will be dealt with first, and which goal he wants to reach first to reduce the problem. Specifying the goal in this way helps to motivate the client to act – it gives something concrete and achievable to work towards. In addition, the course of that action must also be clearly spelt out so as to *enable* the client to act. We will deal with these two points – formulating goals and spelling out the steps – in this section.

Formulating goals

In Chapter 4 we have dealt with the main learning principles, while in various other places the importance of clear goals has been discussed. We will now briefly discuss the considerations that should be taken into account when goals are set.

Specific action

Goals, concrete and accurately described, are a greater stimulus to action than vague ones. A goal such as 'To give meaning to my life' is all well and good, but is not much use for direct action. A more specific and hence usually smaller (sub)goal must therefore be derived from the larger one, for instance to send a letter to the editor on the subject of the abuse of young seals or some other specification on a specific topic. At that level of specific action it becomes possible to indicate the nature and quantity of the effort it takes and to determine when the goal has been reached.

Degrees of difficulty

Goals that are too easy to reach do not stimulate because there is little credit to be gained from them. Unattainable goals, on the other hand, disappoint or deter a client. Hence a golden mean should be found by choosing goals which the client is not afraid to tackle and which will bring him a sense of success when achieved.

Proximity

Though far-off goals regulate the direction of our action, they are less of a stimulus to the action itself. The reward, the satisfaction of reaching the goal, is too far off. The intention to take an exam in three months' time is no stimulant to start today, 'especially when the weather is nice!' But nearer sub-goals do stimulate: 'Today I want to read the first forty pages of this book.' The person can monitor his success quite precisely.

'Ownership'

For a goal to stimulate and motivate, it should be embraced and 'owned'. The person must assume responsibility for it. It is only when a goal is self-chosen that a person will work for it and summon up the necessary courage. This does not mean that initially the goal may not be set by others. The point is whether we ourselves also accept the goal. 'My parents want me to graduate from high school'; this goal will work if I can also say: 'I (myself) want to graduate' which leads to: 'I (myself) will work very hard for the next three months.'

Steps in an action programme

So far we have discussed many aspects of the treatment of problems. We will now describe this whole process in a number of steps. First we will briefly name the various steps, which will then be illustrated by concrete examples.

A method which gives a good overall picture is Egan's (1982) force-field analysis. Which forces contribute to or reduce a problem? What influences play a part? Taking into account the previous analyses in this book and incorporating the force-field analysis, we arrive at ten steps: from the presentation of a problem up to and including the ending of a counselling contact.

1 Identification and clarification of problems

This subject has been fully dealt with, for instance in the problem clarification stage according to Egan's model (discussed in Chapter 5) and with the skills discussed in Chapter 6.

2 Increasing the insight into problems

This was discussed under 'gaining new insights' – the second stage of the counselling model. The skills discussed in Chapter 7 are now added to the helper's arsenal. The client may take it from there with an action programme of his own without outside assistance, or he may accept the existing situation.

3 Priorities

Usually we are faced with more than one problem, or one problem of a complex nature. The question now is which problem (or facet) should be tackled first. Complex problems must be divided into treatable sub-problems which are handled one by one. Client and helper are unlikely to be able to take care of several problems simultaneously. Hence there should be a certain order. In determining the order, the 'worst' problem should not be dealt with first. This problem is usually the hardest to solve. To enhance the client's self-confidence and increase the chance of success, it is useful to start first on a relatively simple (sub)problem.

4 Goals

After selecting a problem the client and helper should formulate outcome goals which can lead to a reduction of the problem. For this the goal-setting principles outlined above are used (p. 164).

5 Means

The next step is to make a survey of the means available to the client to reach his goal. What is he capable of himself? What resources can he call upon? In short, what forces are at his disposal to make the pursuance of his objective easier? Here the question also arises as to how these forces can be reinforced.

On the other side we have the obstructive forces which form a barrier for the fulfilment of the goal. Which factors restrain the client and prevent the goal from being reached? How can these obstructing forces be reduced?

In considering these forces the helper must also help his client in estimating the risks involved. How great is the chance of success? What are the consequences of success or failure? What side-effects can result from the client's actions?

6 Criteria

Helper and client decide together what the outcome of the action must be for it to be called successful. These criteria form a further concretization of the (sub)goals set.

7 Execution

After deciding what action should be taken, the main step now becomes its execution. The client has to do something. To facilitate the execution and make sure that the client will undertake the action adequately, the counsellor might suggest that the proposed action is first carried out in a simulated form, in role-play or imagination. This is followed by the 'homework', with the client carrying out the operation in reality.

8 Evaluation

The client returns to discuss with his 'coach' the experiences he has had with the proposed action. Where has he been successful and where not? What else happened? To what extent has the goal according to the criteria in point 6 been achieved? They will then come to the question of what to do next in view of the results, or lack of them.

9   A new start

On the basis of the evaluation the client will, if necessary, continue to try to reach the goal he has set, or start on a new problem. Depending on the progress made in clarification and differentiation the treatment can begin anew with one of the steps mentioned under points 1–4.

10   The end

When the various cycles in the treatment have been gone through, that is, when the goals have been reached sufficiently or for other reasons (see pp. 172–8), the contact between client and helper is brought to an end.

An example from practice: treatment as education

To illustrate the above ten steps we now give, in a somewhat abbreviated form, an example from practice.

A client, Mrs Jones, comes to see a counsellor, Mr Hall. After a brief introduction by the counsellor about the purpose of this first interview, Mrs Jones says that she suffers from headaches and nervousness. Her doctor has examined her and found no physical causes. He then referred her to the counsellor.

Step 1. Identification and clarification of the problem

The counsellor explains to Mrs Jones that it might be a good idea to find out the possible cause of her nervousness and headaches. What is on her mind? What is happening in her environment? How does she live? It turns out that she is very busy looking after two small children. She is often alone in her flat because her husband is away quite a lot. Moreover, the weekends, which they used to spend quietly in their caravan, are now often disrupted by her parents-in-law. They have recently moved closer to them and they often pay unexpected visits.

Step 2. Acquiring a better insight into the problems

During the discussion it emerges that Mrs Jones has a strong sense of duty. She believes she 'has to' take care of everything in and around the home; she has to please her husband, children, and parents-in-law in her role of friendly housewife. Nevertheless, there are some cracks in her belief. The helper notices a slight irritation: 'Why do I always have to do everything?' Urged by the helper, she admits that there is a problem: namely, that occasionally she would like to do what *she* wants. Specifically, she would first prefer to have a little more peace and quiet, and second to have closer social contacts in the neighbourhood when she wants. But she is afraid to express these wishes, let alone realize them.

Step 3. Priorities

The problems are discussed further and given a preliminary concrete form in two sub-problems: the lack of contact in the neighbourhood and the disruption of the weekends. The first problem is given priority. It is urgent and current, and the action required from the client is within an appropriate range of difficulty. How to reduce the disturbance at the weekends will be dealt with at a later date.

Step 4. Goal

In Mrs Jones' neighbourhood there is a group of housewives who go to a sewing course together, and also visit each other socially. She would very much like to join that 'club'. The first sub-goal is formulated, namely, that she will ask one of the neighbours if she could join them.

Step 5. Means

What will facilitate the reaching of this sub-goal? First impressions are that Mrs Jones rather likes the neighbour in question. She has noticed that this neighbour likes to talk with others, and therefore seems very sociable and approachable. The next question is, does Mrs Jones have the time and opportunities to get to know the neighbour? Now that her two children are at school in the morning, she has more time to spare: the sewing class is also held in the mornings. The few talks with the helper have also made her realize that she can easily keep one morning for herself.

What is now keeping her from reaching the sub-goal of getting in touch with the neighbour? She is not sure how she should address her for she is rather shy. She has doubts whether this sewing class would really suit her. Maybe the other women wouldn't like her to join them, and the neighbour may not want to talk to her. She would be very unhappy about that, for then she would really be alone. Still, she does not want to give up so easily.

Step 6. Criteria

The helper and client agree that in the coming week she will try to achieve two things. She will talk to the neighbour when she meets her next and invite her for a cup of coffee. She thus has a chance to gain two small successes: contact with the nice neighbour and a possible introduction to the sewing class.

Step 7. Execution

The execution appears to be simple, but the helper has some misgivings in view of Mrs Jones' hesitation in making contacts. How can he strengthen the forces which will help her to reach her goal? He discusses the situation with her once more. She has the time to spend one or two mornings away from home; he has her confirm that she also wants that and would enjoy it. The helper looks for a way to reduce the obstructing forces. He suggests that she considers how she might invite the neighbour in for coffee, and then perhaps also broach the subject of the sewing class. The client agrees to that plan, but has trouble with the invitation to the neighbour: 'How do you do that?' The helper proposes that they will rehearse the invitation. The helper will play the role of neighbour and the client will play herself. First they discuss a situation which might be suitable for making the invitation. Mrs Jones mentions that she often meets her neighbour out shopping. So far she has done no more than give a shy nod, but it would be a good moment to address her neighbour. This meeting moment is chosen as the training situation. The client must not only greet the 'neighbour', but also try to engage her in conversation, and invite her to coffee. Helper and client perform this in roleplay several times, with feedback from the helper, until the client is sufficiently confident about the effectiveness of her own performance.

Bolstered by the training and by the positive comments from the helper, the client leaves. In the next session helper and client will evaluate the execution of the plan.

Step 8. Evaluation

A week later client and helper have their next session. How did it go? The first few days the client did not see her neighbour at all! She had begun to doubt if she would succeed. But then, one morning on the way home from her shopping, she had seen her. First she had become frightened ('Now I really have to do it!') but then she had plucked up her courage and stopped her neighbour and invited her over for coffee. To her relief the neighbour's reaction had been positive.

It had been a pleasant visit. She had also introduced the subject of the sewing class. According to the neighbour she was welcome to join; she would take her along next week. In general the carrying-out of her plan had not been as bad as she had feared.

Together client and helper come to the conclusion that the first goal has been reached. The client shows that her first small success has given her greater confidence and courage, though she says: 'It is not all that special. After all, who does not dare to ask something like that of a neighbour?' The helper does not support her in this denigration of her own achievements. First she was afraid to make contact, now she is brave enough; success is success. But there is more to be done, the headaches are not over yet.

Step 9. A new start

Client and helper now go on to the next, rather more difficult subproblem: the disruption of the weekends by the parents-in-law. For this problem steps 2–8 are repeated. In the same way as with the previous problem they first see to what extent the client can alter the situation herself. Does she have the support of her husband? What kind of people are the parents and what does she want herself? Concerning the latter point, she does not want to abandon these old people altogether, they do not have a lot of friends themselves. But she also wants some time on her own and she wants to know where she stands. The talk ends with a plan to seek a compromise with the in-laws. She will try to explain to them that she likes to see them, but that she sometimes feels the need for a quiet weekend and that therefore she would appreciate their calling in advance if and when they are coming over.

This situation, too, is rehearsed by client and helper by simulating the real situation. The helper 'plays' the mother-in-law including the reactions expected (and feared) by the client. The client then carries out the 'homework', and in a subsequent session with her helper, reports success in negotiating with her in-laws some space for herself.

Step 10. Finishing the contact

The progress Mrs Jones has gained from the interviews – creating social contacts plus a few mornings free to pursue her own hobbies away from home, as well as creating enough quiet weekends in the caravan – all contribute to a lessening of her nervousness and head-aches. After some further sessions at longer intervals, designed to help the client hold on to her gains, the contact is finished.

Treatment as education

In the example described above we have not chosen particularly dra-matic or dire problems. Nor is the approach one in which impressive techniques are applied. We have chosen to do this not just to provide a straightforward illustration, but also because we want to stress that many personal problems begin 'simply' and, provided they are noted in time, can also be solved 'simply'.

We write 'simply' in inverted commas, because one should not be fooled by this simplicity. When the helper's approach to the client is even slightly amiss, things may go wrong. When for instance, he thinks 'Well, to get in touch with the neighbour, that can't be such a big problem' and fails to find out how the client would actually go about doing that, there is every chance of the whole plan falling through. It is even doubtful if the client would have the courage to come back to the helper when she fails to accomplish such a 'simple' task. Also, the process of gaining insight into one's own wishes and 'duties' is very necessary as a preparation to action and requires a great deal of empathy from the counsellor in assessing where the client gets stuck. Is it her own doing? How far does the environment play a role and what are the underlying wishes of the client? Finally, we deliberately chose a problem that can be treated by a combination of gaining insight and individual training in social skills. There are strong indications (Ivey and Authier 1978; Argyle 1981; Patterson 1986) that many personal problems that cause clients to seek help are the result of a lack of positive relationships. Often such clients do not have any friends with whom they can discuss their problems. One of the first questions a helper should ask himself is: why does this client come to me and why does he not go to someone in his own environment? Showing a client the way to these possibilities is often a better and more obvious way of helping than offering him lengthy professional counselling.

The procedure we have discussed in the foregoing example from practice is inspired by the idea that with personal problems treat-ment should be considered as a form of education (Authier, Gustafson, Guerney, and Kasdorf 1975). The client is seen as someone with a few shortcomings in his knowledge and skills related to his way of living which have led to problems. Therefore the solution lies in overcoming these shortcomings by means of teaching psychological insights and social skills which are directly applicable to the client's personal situation. The cooperation between client and helper in his role of teacher and coach prevents the client from viewing this education as authoritarian or manipulative. Moreover, the educational model of helping lowers the threshold for potential clients. They need not bear the stigma of being considered problematic or sick (Szasz 1960). Several investigations have shown that well-prepared training courses in social skills are effective in enabling clients to improve their social contacts (Ivey and Authier 1978; Van der Molen, 1985; L'Abate and Milan 1985).

Termination

It is simpler to begin counselling than to end it. Personal problems are frequently quite complicated; one problem leads to another. This means that it is not so simple to decide when the helper can or must end his part in the counselling. Moreover, in the course of counselling a certain bond is created which is sometimes hard to break for both parties. To conclude this book we will therefore discuss several aspects of the ending of the contact between helper and client.

Referral

One way in which the contact is frequently ended is by referral. By this we mean that the client is referred to another counsellor or institution on the initiative of the helper, who is no longer able or willing to continue the counselling.

Referral has a bad name among clients. A frequently heard complaint is: 'They just send you from pillar to post.' Clients are convinced that they are unwanted guests who should be got rid of. The helper redirects the client without telling him much about the reason behind that. We therefore suggest a way of referring which may help to diminish the negative experiences of the client.

Referring the client can be seen as a special sort of action programme which runs mainly according to the steps mentioned on pp. 165–7. At a certain moment – and that can be at any time during the counselling process – the helper comes to the conclusion that the problems can be solved better by referring the client to someone else. The action then consists of this referral being accomplished with a maximum of openness and collaboration with the client. To that end the helper must:

- tell the client that he wants to refer him;
- explain why he wants to do this;
- tell him to whom he wants to refer him and what the client is likely to expect there;
- make an appointment with the client to view together whether the referral has gone according to plan.

Let us briefly comment on these parts of the referral.

When the helper is of the opinion that it is better to refer the client to someone else, he will have to tell him that. Usually the reason is that the other person is better able to help the client.

The helper has to explain why and to whom he will refer his client. In order to reduce the client's uncertainty to a minimum the helper makes sure that his explanation is clear and concrete. It is very important that the helper is fully alive to his client's reactions. Since the referral is also in his interest, the helper will be eager to convince the client, and in doing so will often fail to listen closely to the content and background of the client's objections.

When the client has had time to consider the referral he is faced with the choice whether to take it up or not. In some cases it may be necessary to give the client more time to think this over, and break off the counselling for the time being. When the referral is accepted, the time has come to discuss practical matters: how to begin the new contact, how to get there, etc. With many clients this, too, should be dealt with in a practical manner.

Finally, there is the supervision of the referral. A properly executed action programme includes evaluation. For the referral this means that it is very important after the referral session for the helper to have one more contact (brief, or by telephone) with the client to learn what has happened. Has the client gone to the address in question? Were his experiences in accordance with his expectations? Is the client going to be helped further?

This final contact serves several purposes. The former counsellor demonstrates to his client that he is not suddenly abandoning him. The overlap assures the client that the old relationship is not gone before a new one is created. The helper gets a chance to hear if all went well with his client. Often the referring is also difficult for the helper because he is not sure if his client is better off elsewhere and if this help will be adequate. Finally, this contact after the referral can serve as a stimulus for the client to go to the referral address; after all, he has to report on this later on.

The client does not want to go on

An easy way in which the client can show that he no longer desires contact with the helper is not to appear at the appointed time. This method leaves the helper with a great many unanswered questions, as well as feeling angry, disappointed, or sad.

We think it important that the client should not be abandoned after having acted in this way. Whereas with friends or acquaintances who behave thus we are inclined to think, 'Well, I'm not going to run after him, it is up to him now to make the first move,' this is not the right attitude with clients. After all, there may be many reasons for failing to appear which may not be due to unwillingness on the part of the client: he is afraid, the helper has gone too fast, the client does not like the helper personally and he does not know how to show this except by not showing up; new difficulties have arisen which the client may be unable to explain to his helper; the client didn't do his 'homework' and is ashamed of that. In view of all this, it is up to the helper at least to get in touch with the client one more time and invite him again for a talk, if only to find out for himself what motivated the client and show that he has every right to end the contact. The acceptance of the client as a person with his own idiosyncrasies demands this. This point of view implies that the helper should not jump to conclusions, for example, that the client is no longer 'motivated' and that therefore there is nothing left for him to do.

Another difficulty occurs when the helper and the client have different views on whether to continue the contact. The client thinks it has been sufficient and he can now manage alone. The helper, on the other hand, believes that the contact should be continued because the outcome goals they have set have not yet been reached. To what extent should the helper give priority to the client's own rights and wishes?

Before trying to answer this the helper should ask himself what is behind the client's request to end the contact. The reason may be one of the following:

- I don't like your way of helping.
- Though you say you want to help me, I don't trust you; when I say I want to stop and you agree immediately, I know that I was right not to trust you.
- I think my problems cannot be solved anyway, so let's just call it quits.
- All these things you ask me to do as 'homework' frighten me, but I am also afraid to say so.

But perhaps the client actually does mean: 'I want to finish now. Though the agreed-upon goal has not quite been reached, I can manage alone from now on!'

Whatever the reason, the helper here finds himself in the dilemma discussed in Chapter 2 between leaving free or influencing. On the one hand, people should be allowed the freedom to go their own way, and should be given that freedom fully and taken at their word. On the other hand, if one has a close relationship with and responsibility for a fellow human being, one does not just let him do something when one thinks it will be harmful to him.

One approach is to discuss the dilemma openly with the client. This clears the way for the helper in good conscience to voice his objection to a premature finishing of the contact. Having done this, the helper may well find that this is the very thing the client had been hoping for – that is, to hear the helper object to termination at this time. Indeed, if the helper *fails* to voice his objection in this way, he may leave the client thinking, 'You see, I'm not worth the trouble, he also wants to be rid of me, just like everyone else.' It may be, though, that the client really does not want any more help (at least from this helper). That is the client's right and, of course, the helper should respect his decision: at the most he can offer to leave the door open (in case the client should change his mind) or help him to find another counsellor.

The helper does not want to go on

The helper does not want to continue counselling, but the client does. This, too, may happen. We will sketch some situations with the reasons for the helper's standpoint.

The helper believes that the *goals* of counselling have been sufficiently *reached* and he therefore wants to stop. The client, however, disagrees and wants more help for the same problem or has other difficulties. This difference of opinion forces the helper to make a choice: does he keep to his point of view and terminate or does he go on? This, then, becomes a subject of discussion between client and helper to find out what the motives of the client are.

A second circumstance in which it is better that the helper does not continue with a particular client, is when he finds that he and the client are *totally incompatible*, resulting in strong feelings of antipathy. Such feelings are not conducive to a profitable cooperation. Even more important, they can lead to the client not being adequately helped or ending up with even greater problems. This does not mean that a helper should decide to end the contact after the first negative reaction. Often a client changes when the relation has become more confiding. His 'mask' which caused the helper's antipathy, is no longer needed and is dropped. Perhaps, too, the helper's feelings toward his client change when he hears more about the client's background. Moreover, it is the helper's task to help someone as best he can, which requires some detachment from the client as a person and from his idiosyncrasies. Furthermore, it is important for the helper to find out whether his aversion is caused by certain demonstrable characteristics of the client or is based on a general feeling of discomfort. In the former case the helper could point these out at a suitable moment to the client in a direct way. The client may learn something from this.

Another factor that may hamper the counselling relationship is *strong positive feelings*, for instance when the helper falls in love. This makes it impossible for him to keep the necessary distance from his client, while the powerful feelings will also make it hard for him to 'think straight'. When these strong negative or positive sentiments of the helper persist and thereby remain an obstacle, it is in the interest of both client and helper to break off the professional relationship. The helper will have to tell his client this. It is always a point of discussion whether the true reason should be clearly stated or if the helper may invent an acceptable excuse. In such a situation frankness is not always in the client's interest, for instance when this frankness would be too shocking or disappointing. (This last remark is not, however, meant to give the helper licence to choose the easiest way out.)

Another reason for the helper to break the contact is when the *differences between* his own *norms and values* and those of the client are too wide. This may reveal itself when the goal that the client wants to achieve is unacceptable to the helper.

For example, a client, a soldier, wants to learn to get on 'better' with his subordinates by manipulating them through a clever use of social skills. Another client, a teacher, has problems with his pupils but does not want to give up his consistently anti-authoritarian and extremely liberal way of teaching. In such cases the helper can get into a situation where he is no longer willing to cooperate with the intentions of his client. The helper is clearly entitled to certain limits where the acceptance of other people's views are concerned. A 'straight' talk between both parties may lead to a mutually agreed ending of the counselling.

Finally, an important and frequently occurring reason for the helper to end the contact is when he considers himself to *lack the expertise* to help the client with his problem. In the introduction in Chapter 1 we mentioned that the clients we have in mind are accessible clients with an as yet unspecified problem who turn to a counsellor. So it is quite probable that during the stage of problem clarification they ask for help that the counsellor does not feel able to offer. Or, it may turn out during the treatment stage that other help should be sought because the goals have not been reached and are unlikely to be. Even when the client is eager to continue with counselling, it is the helper's responsibility to make a judgement and end the contact if necessary.

In all these cases where the helper is unwilling or unable to continue with his client, possibilities for referral should obviously be considered and discussed.

The goal has been reached

We end now by discussing the happy situation where the goal of counselling has been reached and counselling can come to a natural end. This ending, too, needs to be effected appropriately, and it is important that it does not come unexpectedly. The method demonstrated in the steps of the action programme mentioned on pp. 165–7 contains various points at which an acceptable conclusion can be effected. The first point is a guideline for determining the goal of the counselling. When the goal has been reached, the contact is concluded.

An awkward point is that most outcome goals are sub-goals of a more general one. When loneliness is the problem, 'learning how to develop social contacts' is a sub-goal of 'overcoming loneliness'. But when are the contacts sufficiently frequent and satisfying for the loneliness to be said to be adequately solved? Frequently the questions in personal problems cannot be clearly answered. Therefore, the evaluation of what has been accomplished should also include a discussion about ending or continuing the contact. The question, then, is not whether the problems have been completely solved or general goals reached, but whether the client is capable of continuing by himself thanks to the insight (and skills) he has acquired.

The helper should always try to choose this moment as early as possible. This serves to prevent the client from becoming increasingly dependent. The longer the contact continues, the more the client becomes used to the helper's support. We remind readers of the fact that usually the client has already been working on his problems prior to his contact with the helper. Then, after getting some assistance from the counsellor, he has to manage by himself again. This time he may be better equipped to tackle his problems and better able to use the resources in his environment. Counselling is only a temporary aid to help the client, to prevent or treat his problems in life. During the termination stage of the contact, the helper should make this view of his work clear to the client. Often practical matters, such as the time available, or finances, will also play a part. The time for the final session, however, should be settled long before by mutual agreement.

It is by no means necessary for counselling to end abruptly. When the transition between 'everything' and 'nothing' is too great, the client may try to put off the ending of the contact. A compromise can be found by letting the last few sessions be held at longer intervals, and also by keeping the door open after the final session. This background security sometimes gives the client a sufficient sense of reassurance to face life alone better.

Videotapes

Two colour video training films . . . . .

Introductory
Counselling Skills
and
Pitfalls in the
Counselling Process

made by

**The Department of Psychology
University of Leicester (U.K.)
and
The Department of Personality Psychology
University of Groningen (The Netherlands)**

The first film, Introductory Counselling Skills, includes demonstrations
of nine major skills which have been empirically established as basic
to good counselling.

The second film, Pitfalls in the Counselling Process, contains
demonstrations of six difficult interactions in the counselling process.

In each case the client and counsellor are roleplayed and a helpful
and an unhelpful version of each skill is shown. The films are
organised in a way to facilitate their use in workshop format.
A manual is also available, which provides step by step guidance in
the organisation of a training course.

**To be ordered from :
Department of Clinical Psychology,
University of Leicester,
University Road, Leicester LE1 7RH**   Tel: 0533-522522 Ext. 2481

Available on VHS format

VHS Prices **Film 1 – £90.00   Film 2 – £75.00   Manual – £4.00**

References

Argyle, M. (1981) *Social Skills and Health*, London: Methuen.

Authier, J., Gustafson, K., Guerney, B.J., and Kasdorf, J. (1975) 'The psychological practitioner as a teacher: a theoretical-historical and practical review', *The Counselling Psychologist*, 5: 31–50.

Bandler, J. and Grinder, R. (1975) *The Structure of Magic, I*, Palo Alto: Science and Behavior.

Bandura, A. (1977) *Social Learning Theory*, Englewood Cliffs, New Jersey: Prentice Hall.

Bandura, A. (1986) *Social Foundations of Thought and Action. A Social Cognitive Theory*, Englewood Cliffs, New Jersey: Prentice Hall.

Barendregt, J.T. (1982) *De Zielenmarkt. Over Psychotherapie in alle Ernst*, Meppel: Boom.

Beauvoir, S. de (1948) *The Ethics of Ambiguity*, Secaucus, New Jersey: Citadel Press. Translated from *Pour une morale de l'ambiguité*, Paris: Gallimard, 1947.

Beck, A.T., Rush, A.J., Shaw, B.F., and Emery, G. (1979) *Cognitive Therapy of Depression*, New York: The Guilford Press.

Bellak, L. and Small, L. (1978) *Emergency Psychotherapy and Brief Psychotherapy*, London: Grune & Stratton.

Benjamin, A. (1969) *The Helping Interview*, Boston, Mass.: Houghton Mifflin.

Berenson, B.G. and Mitchell, K.M. (1976) *Confronting for Better or Worse*, Amherst, Mass.: Human Resource Development Press.

Bierkens, P.B. (1976) *Woord en Communicatie. Gespreksvoering in Theorie en Praktijk*, Nijmegen: Dekker & Van de Vegt.

Brayfield, A.H. (1962) 'Performance is the thing', *Journal of Counseling Psychology*, 9: 3.

Butcher, J.N. and Koss, M.P. (1978) 'Research on brief and crisis-oriented therapies', in S.L. Garfield and A.E. Bergin (eds) *Handbook of Psychotherapy and Behavior Change. An Empirical Analysis*, New York: Wiley & Sons.

Carkhuff, R.R. (1969a) *Helping and Human Relations I: Selection and Training*, New York: Holt, Rinehart & Winston.

Carkhuff, R.R. (1969b) *Helping and Human Relations. II: Practice and Research*, New York: Holt, Rinehart & Winston.

Carkhuff, R.R. and Berenson, B.G. (1967) *Beyond Counseling and Therapy*, New York: Holt, Rinehart & Winston.

Chomsky, N. (1965) *Aspects of the Theory of Syntax*, Cambridge, Mass.: MIT Press.

Chomsky, N. (1968) *Language and Mind*, New York: Harcourt, Brace, Jovanovitch.

Duijker, H.C.J. (1978) 'Competentie en verantwoordelijkheid van de psycholoog', *Nederlands Tijdschrift voor de Psychologie*, 33: 497–511.

Duijker, H.C.J. (1980) *Psychopolis. Een essay over de beoefening der psychologie*, Deventer: Van Loghum Slaterus.

Egan, G. (1975) *The Skilled Helper. A Model for Systematic Helping and Interpersonal Relating*, Monterey, California: Brooks/Cole Publishing Company.

Egan, G. (1982) *The Skilled Helper. Model, Skills and Methods for Effective Helping. Second Edition*, Monterey, California: Brooks/Cole Publishing Company.

Ellis, A. (1974) *Humanistic Psychotherapy. The Rational-Emotive Approach*, New York: McGraw Hill.

Festinger, L. (1954a) 'Motivations of compliant behavior', in M.R.Jones (ed.) *Nebraska Symposium on Motivation*, Lincoln, Nebraska: University of Nebraska Press.

Festinger, L. (1954b) 'A theory of social comparison processes', *Human Relations*, 7: 117–40.

Frijda, N.H. (1986) *The Emotions*, Cambridge: Cambridge University Press.

Garfield, S.L. (1982) 'Eclecticism and integrationism in psychotherapy', *Behavior Therapy*, 13: 610–23.

Goldstein, A.P. (1973) *Structured Learning Therapy. Toward a Psychotherapy for the Poor*, New York: Academic Press.

Greenspoon, J. (1955) 'The reinforcing effect of two spoken sounds on the frequency of two responses', *American Journal of Psychology*, 68: 409–16.

Groot, A.D. de (1975) 'Categories of educational objectives and effect measures: a new approach discussed in the context of second-language learning', in A.J. van Essen and J.F. Hunting (eds) *The Context of Foreign-language Learning*, Assen: Van Gorcum, 30–70.

Groot A.D. de (1978) *Thought and Choice in Chess*, The Hague: Mouton & Co.

Hackney, H. and Cormier, L.S. (1979) *Counseling Strategies and Objectives*, Englewood Cliffs, New Jersey: Prentice Hall.

Hall, C.S. and Lindzey, G. (1978) *Theories of Personality*, New York: Wiley & Sons.

Hergenhahn, B.R. (1984) *An Introduction to Theories of Personality*, Englewood Cliffs, New Jersey: Prentice Hall.

Ivey, A.E. (1971) *Microcounseling. Innovations in Interviewing Training*, Springfield, Illinois: Charles C. Thomas.

Ivey, A.E. and Authier, J. (1978) *Microcounseling. Innovations in Interviewing, Counseling, Psychotherapy and Psychoeducation*, Springfield, Illinois:

Charles C. Thomas.

James, W. (1962) *Talks to Teachers on Psychology and to Students on some of Life's Ideals*, New York: Dover Publications (orig. pub. New York: Hall & Co., 1899).

Kagan, N. (1975) *Influencing Human Interaction*, Washington, DC: American Personnel and Guidance Association.

Knapp, M.L. (1978) *Non-verbal Communication in Human Interaction* (2nd edn), New York: Holt, Rinehart & Winston.

Koch, S. (1971) 'The image of man implicit in encounter group theory', *Journal of Humanistic Psychology*, 11: 109–28.

Korsch, B.M. and Negrete, V.F. (1972) 'Doctor-patient communication', *Scientific American*, 227: 66–74.

Kouwer, B.J. (1973) *Existentiële psychologie. Grondslagen van het Psychologisch Gesprek*, Meppel: Boom.

L'Abate, L. and Milan, M.A. (eds) (1985) *Handbook of Social Skills Training and Research*, New York: John Wiley & Sons.

Lange, A. (1980) 'Positief etiketteren. Een aanvulling', in K. van der Velden (ed.), *Directieve Therapie* 2, Deventer: Van Loghum Slaterus.

Levy, L.H. (1963) *Psychological Interpretation*, New York: Holt, Rinehart & Winston.

Lewin, K. (1958) 'Group decision and social change', in E. Maccoby, T. Newcomb, and E. Hartley (eds) *Readings in Social Psychology* (3rd edn), New York: Holt, Rinehart & Winston.

Matarazzo, R.G., Philips, J.S., Wiens, A.N., and Saslow, G. (1965) 'Learning the art of interviewing. A study of what beginning students do and their patterns of change', *Psychotherapy*, 2: 49–60.

Mehrabian, A. (1972) *Non-verbal Communication*, Chicago: Aldine.

Mischel, W. (1968) *Personality and Assessment*, New York: Wiley & Sons.

Mischel, W. (1973) 'Toward a cognitive social learning reconceptualization of personality', *Psychological Review*, 80: 252–83.

Molen, H.T. van der (1985) *Hulp als Onderwijs. Effecten van Cursussen voor Verlegen Mensen*, Gröningen: Wolters-Noordhoff.

Nelson-Jones, R. (1982) *The Theory and Practice of Counselling Psychology*, London: Holt, Rinehart & Winston.

Pannekoek, Y. (1982) *Memoires*, Amsterdam: C.A. van Oorschot.

Patterson, C.H. (1986) *Theories of Counseling and Psychotherapy*, New York: Harper & Row.

Rogers, C.R. (1951) *Client-Centred Therapy. Its Current Practice, Implications and Theory*, London: Constable.

Rogers, C.R. (1957) 'The necessary and sufficient conditions of therapeutic personality change', *Journal of Consulting Psychology*, 21: 95–103.

Rogers, C.R. (1959) 'A theory of therapy, personality, and interpersonal relationships, as developed in the client-centered framework', in S. Koch, (ed.) *Psychology: A Study of a Science, 3: Formulations of the Person and the Social Context*, New York: McGraw Hill.

Rogers, C.R. (1961) *On Becoming a Person*, Boston, Mass.: Houghton Mifflin.

Rogers, C.R. (1962) 'The interpersonal relationship: the core of guidance',

Harvard Educational Review, 32: 416–29.

Shapiro, D.A. and Shapiro, D. (1982) 'Meta-analysis of comparative therapy outcome studies: a replication and refinement', *Psychological Bulletin*, 92: 581–604.

Skinner, B.F. (1948) *Walden Two*, New York: Macmillan.

Skinner, B.F. (1953) *Science and Human Behavior*, New York: Macmillan.

Smith, M.L. and Glass, G.V. (1977) 'Meta-analysis of psychotherapy outcome studies', *American Psychologist*, 32: 752–60.

Szasz, T.S. (1960) 'The myth of mental illness', *The American Psychologist*, 15: 113–18.

Trower, P., Casey, A., and Dryden, W. (1988) *Cognitive Behavioural Counselling in Action*, London: Sage Publications Ltd.

Truax, Ch.B. (1966) 'Reinforcement and nonreinforcement in Rogerian psychotherapy', *Journal of Abnormal Psychology*, 71 (1): 1–9.

Wachtel, P. (1977) *Psychoanalysis and Behavior Therapy: Toward an Integration*, New York: Basic Books.

Watzlawick, P., Beavin, J.H., and Jackson, D.D. (1967) *Pragmatics of Human Communications*, New York: Norton.

Wexler, D.A. (1974) 'A cognitive theory of experiencing, self-actualization, and therapeutic process', in D.A. Wexler and L.N. North Rice (eds) *Innovations in Client-Centered Therapy*, New York: Wiley & Sons.

Wills, T.A. (1978) 'Perceptions of clients by professional helpers', *Psychological Bulletin*, 85: 968–1000.

Author index

Argyle, M. 171, 181
Authier, J. 171, 172, 181, 182

Bandler, J. 117,181
Bandura, A. 2, 24, 41, 42, 44, 48,
    67, 70, 135, 140, 181
Barendregt, J.T. 160, 181
Beauvoir, S. de 11, 181
Beavin, J.H. 97, 184
Beck, A.T. 62, 181
Bellak, L. 4, 181
Benjamin, A. 131, 181
Berenson, B.G. 79, 80, 76, 146–9,
    181, 182
Bergin, A.E. 181
Bierkens, P.B. 133, 181
Brayfield, A.H. 32, 181
Butcher, J.N. 77, 181

Carkhuff, R.R. 2, 79, 80, 154, 181,
    182
Casey, A. 30, 184
Chomsky, N. 117, 182
Cormier, L.S. 55, 98, 101, 110, 182

Dryden, W. 30, 184
Duijker, H.C.J. 81, 82, 182

Egan, G. 2, 69, 79, 80, 90, 94, 116,
    144–8, 154, 165, 182
Ellis, A. 33, 51, 122, 160, 182
Emery, G. 62, 181

Essen, A.J. van 182

Festinger, L. 49, 182
Frijda, N.H. 37, 182

Garfield, S.L. 2, 181, 182
Glass, G.V. 23, 184
Goldstein, A.P. 31, 184
Greenspoon, J. 100, 182
Grinder, R. 117, 181
Groot, A.D. de 89, 182
Guerney, B.J. 172, 181
Gustafson, K. 171, 181

Hackney, H. 55, 98, 101, 110, 182
Hall, C.S. 23, 182
Hartley, E. 183
Hergenhahn, B.R. 23, 182
Hunting, J.F. 182

Ivey, A.E. 90, 91, 154, 171, 172, 182

Jackson, D.D. 97, 184
James, W. 65, 183
Jones, M.R. 182

Kagan, N. 130, 183
Kasdorf, J. 172, 181
Knapp, M.L. 98, 183
Koch, S. 39, 183
Korsch, B.M. 16, 183
Koss, M.P. 77, 181

Author index

Kouwer, B.J. 124, 183
L'Abate, L. 172, 183
Lange, A. 150, 183
Levy, L.H. 136, 137, 142, 183
Lewin, K. 15, 77, 183
Lindzey, G. 23, 182

Maccoby, E. 183
Matarazzo, R.G. 92, 183
Mehrabian, A. 97, 183
Milan, M.A. 172, 183
Mischel, W. 2, 24, 41, 122, 183
Mitchell, K.M. 146–9, 181
Molen, H.T. van der 172, 183

Negrete, V.F. 16, 183
Nelson-Jones, R. 148, 183
Newcomb, T. 183
North-Rice, L.N. 184

Pannekoek, Y. 161, 183
Patterson, C.H. 33, 171, 183
Philips, J.S. 92, 183

Rogers, C.R. 2, 24–35, 37, 38, 40,
    41, 57, 66, 78–80, 137, 183, 184
Rush, A.J. 62, 181

Saslow, G. 92, 183
Shapiro, D. 23, 184
Shapiro, D.A. 23, 184
Shaw, B.F. 62, 181
Skinner, B.F. 31, 184
Small, L. 4, 181
Smith, M.L. 23, 184
Szasz, T.S. 172, 184

Trower, P. 30, 160, 184
Truax, Ch.B. 30, 184

Velden, K. van der 183

Wachtel, P. 2, 184
Watzlawick, P. 97, 184
Wexler, D.A. 2, 24, 34, 35, 37–40,
    58, 59, 61, 71, 135, 184
Wiens, A.N. 92, 183
Wills, T.A. 82, 116, 184

Subject index

acceptance 25, 26, 58, 78, 98, 110, 112, 160–3, 174, 177; unconditional 18, 57
accessibility 3
action 40, 45–7, 57, 66, 70, 74–7, 119, 127, 162–4, 166, 168, 171; plan(s) 31, 159; programme(s) 74, 144, 158, 165, 172, 173, 177; goal-directed 163
advanced accurate empathy 142–4
advice 1, 8, 13-19, 77, 91, 117, 133; giving 77, 91
anonymity 84
antecedents 119, 120
anxiety 38, 59, 63, 91, 100, 117, 129, 160
approach: client-centred 23, 24, 29, 30, 135; social learning 41
assertiveness skills 45
asymmetrical relation 83
attending behaviour 84, 92
attention 17, 26, 40, 44, 61, 69, 70, 74, 77, 94–7, 99, 102, 106, 110–12, 115, 149
attentiveness 17
attitude: typical of friends and relatives 7
authoritarian leadership style 39
authority 104
aversion 176
avoidance behaviour(s) 47, 67, 101

bad news 91, 128
basic attitude 91
beginner's mistakes 103
behaviourist theory 32
blushing 113
body language 99
breathing 95

choice 7, 18, 19, 30, 74, 111; of words 140
clarification 73, 75, 94, 128, 158, 167
clarity 36, 54, 64, 69, 77, 94, 116, 122
classification 60, 61
client-centred 2, 20, 23, 24, 29, 30, 34, 61, 91, 135; theory 2
coach 66–8, 73, 166, 172
codes of practice for clinical psychologists 81
cognitive behavioural therapy 160
cognitive process(es) 33, 44, 46, 160
cognitive psychology 2, 32, 34
cognitive system 137
cognitive theory 41; of experiencing 34
commonalities in processes of helping 2
common sense 81, 95
compensating function 152
concreteness 92, 116, 126
concretization 102
conditional regard 26, 28

confidant 57–60, 66, 67, 137
confidence 70, 99
confrontation 142, 144–9, 156, 157;
    action 149; strength 148;
    weakness 148, 149
congruence 27, 78, 157
congruity 57
consequences 20, 45–7, 119, 120;
    positive 45; negative 45
content aspect of communication 97
contract 92, 93, 95, 122, 124, 125;
    initial 93, 95, 122, 125
control 159–62; levels of 159
conversation 7, 10, 14, 15, 17, 54,
    56, 62, 66, 96, 97, 101, 103, 106,
    109, 110, 112, 115, 122, 124,
    129, 130, 143
cooperation 16–21, 33, 69, 94, 95,
    115, 122, 125, 126, 128–30, 135,
    154, 172, 176; model 16–21, 54,
    59, 95, 122, 125, 126, 129, 135
counselling as a way of life 79
counselling model 165
crisis 93; intervention 76
criteria 166, 169

degrees of difficulty 164
depersonalization experiences 160
depression 39, 53, 62
depth structure 117
detection 61
detective 61–7, 70, 137, 140;
    communicative 60, 64
dexterity 31
diagnosis 60
diagnosis–prescription
    approach/model 12, 15–17,
    19–21, 77
diagnostic category 139
dialogue 4, 7, 9, 94, 105, 124, 128
differentiation 36, 37, 61–3, 71, 117,
    167
dilemma 11, 18, 19, 81, 175
direct mutual communication 154
directive 11, 15
directiveness 93
directivity 32
directness 99, 142, 154–7

discrepancy/cies 147, 148
disponere 89
disposition 89; behavioural 89
distance 20, 83, 85, 124, 153
doorhandle phenomenon 133

eclectic 2
effective(ness) 2, 23, 77
efficacy expectations 48, 67
emotionality 152
emotions 10, 37–40, 58, 98, 115,
    122, 128, 143, 144, 152
empathy 28-30, 58, 66, 78, 84, 112,
    142, 171
empirical research 23
encouraging gestures 99
ending the counselling interview
    122, 131, 132
environment 4, 26, 31, 32, 41–3, 49,
    63, 67, 68, 145, 151, 159, 167,
    171, 178
evaluation 132, 166, 167, 169, 173,
    178
examples of one's own 128, 142,
    153, 154, 156, 157
execution (of plans) 166, 169
existentialism 11, 24
existentialist philosophy 24; view 17
expectancy/cies 47; influencing 48
expectations 47, 48, 68, 93, 95, 124,
    125, 128, 130, 154, 159, 173;
    influence of 47; mutual 124,
    125, 130
experiential world 18, 20, 28, 63–5,
    70, 81, 84
expert 15, 18, 20, 21, 59, 140
expertise 21, 48, 78, 126, 139, 177
exploration 70, 71, 74, 75, 101, 108,
    113, 143, 163
external factors 43, 48, 49
eye contact 99, 110

facial expression 28, 97–9
feedback 98, 130, 169
feelings 18, 20, 21, 26–9, 31, 34, 37,
    38, 40, 48, 59, 63, 70, 92, 94,
    111–15, 120–2, 126, 138, 143,
    144, 147, 152, 153, 156, 176;

complex 113; of antipathy 176; of control 48; simple 113; strong positive 176
flexibility 21, 110
follow-up interview 57
force-field analysis 165
frame of reference 1, 15, 20, 61, 94, 104, 106, 108, 129, 130, 134, 136–8, 142, 145, 154
freedom 10, 11, 15, 18, 29, 41, 106, 175; of choice 11
frowning 98

games 148
genuine(ness) 21, 22, 27, 28, 33, 58, 98, 110
gestures 28, 99
goal 2, 47, 49, 50, 51, 54–6, 69, 72–4, 77, 78, 89, 90–2, 109, 119, 123–5, 131, 132, 134, 151, 154, 159, 163–8, 170, 175, 177, 178; intention 90; operational 90; outcome 55, 56, 69, 123, 165; process 55, 56, 123; specific 90
goal-evaluation 92, 122, 123, 131
goal-setting 92, 122, 123
goodness 32
group activities 39
growth 41, 62, 79

haste, hastiness 76, 77
helper as a person 2, 78
helping model 54, 68, 69, 74, 85, 133
here-and-now situation 154
homework 166, 170, 174, 175
humanistic-psychological literature 79
humour 84

ideal-image 50, 52, 53, 138, 139; tyranny of 50, 85
identification of problem(s) 165, 167
immediacy 154
incongruence 26, 27, 98
information 15, 16, 32, 72, 76, 102, 120; coding of 32; giving of 77, 141; interpretation of 35, 36; processing 32, 35–41, 58, 59, 65;

processor 47; selection of 62; storing of 32, 44
informing function 46
insight(s) 3, 4, 18, 20, 31, 32, 37, 55, 57, 58, 61, 66–8, 70–3, 76, 77, 81, 94, 135, 137, 138, 142, 143, 149, 154, 155, 158, 159, 162, 163, 167, 172, 178; deepening of 71; gaining new 4, 70, 72, 90, 94, 133, 134, 136, 147, 158, 165, 171
insightful connections 135
integration 24, 36, 37, 58, 61–3, 71
internal factors 49
internalization 26
Interpersonal Process Recall method 130
interpersonal skills 48
interpretation 46, 65, 70, 75, 135–42, 144, 153; as a skill 137; psychological 136, 141; re-interpretation 137
intervention 57; minimal 57
interview 54, 55, 57, 69, 90–3, 95, 103, 104, 114, 122, 125, 131, 132, 137, 138, 154, 156; duration of 131
interviewing techniques 90
intonation 97, 113
involvement 84, 95, 98

language 36, 110, 116, 140, 141
learning: by example 45; of behaviour 41; from consequences 45; principles 43, 163; process(es) 31, 41–3, 47
learning theory/theoretical 23
lengthy treatment 77
listening behaviour 103
looking 99
love 11, 12, 25, 26

manipulation 20, 21
mask(s) 145, 176
means 166, 168
mental attitude 94
memory 44, 120
meta-conversation 124, 128, 131, 132

minimal encouragement(s) 100,
105, 110, 129
mirroring 30
mixing of roles 128
model 15–21, 54, 59, 75–7, 90, 94,
95, 138, 149; cooperation *see*
cooperation model; counselling
94; developmental 90;
diagnosis–prescription *see*
diagnosis–prescription model;
helping 54, 68, 69, 74, 85, 133;
interviewing 90, 138, 149;
three-stage 94, 95
modelling 43
modelling function 156
motivating function 46
motivation 9, 12, 43, 44, 46, 50
muscle tension 113

naming 159, 160, 163
necessary conditions 80
negative self-image 151
negotiating process 94
newsprint 144
nod(ding) 26, 99
non-directiveness 30, 34, 93
non-verbal behaviour 97, 142
non-verbal channels 97
non-verbal message 98
norm(s) 26, 32, 80, 81, 151, 152,
162, 176; system of 18
nuance(s) 36, 58, 62, 63, 70, 110

object of research 14, 18
objectivity 81
observation 65
openness 129, 172
order 91, 122, 159
outcome expectations 48, 67
outcome goal(s) 55, 56, 69, 123, 165
overconcern 12
ownership 164

paraphrases/paraphrasing of
content 92, 109, 110–13, 116,
117, 120, 125, 126, 139, 142
parrot: act like a 30
passivity 20

pattern of expectation 133
perception 43
perceptual processes 35
personality 33, 43, 65, 82; factors
24; theory 23, 33, 136, 138
philosophy of the helper 12
phobia 160
pitfalls 83, 128
plans: execution of 77
positive relabelling 142, 149, 150–3
posture 28, 99, 110, 113
preconceptions 111
prejudice(s) 65, 82, 152
priorities 165, 168
problem clarification 69, 70, 89, 90,
94, 104, 109, 112, 115, 116, 119,
123, 133–5, 137, 165, 167, 177
process goal 55, 56, 123
professional distortion 82
professional peer group 96
proximity 164
punishment 49–51

questionnaires 142
questions: asking 14, 76, 92, 106,
118, 129; closed 106, 108, 109,
116; goal-evaluation 123; open
104, 106, 107, 109, 116, 139;
suggestive 108; why 109

rapport 69, 70
rational-emotive therapy 160
receptivity 40
reciprocity 83
recognition of feeling(s) 115
reconstruction 149, 150
referral 172–4, 177
reflection of feeling/reflecting 29,
30, 90, 92, 111–17, 120, 125–8,
134, 142
reinforcement 111
reinforcer(s) 31
relational aspect of communication
97
relativization 84, 85
repertoire 109
repertoire of behaviours 47
responsibility 10–12, 17, 18, 32, 72,

73, 91, 93, 126, 147, 148, 164, 175, 177
reward 49, 50, 164
role 2, 15, 57, 58, 60, 61, 64, 65, 68–70, 73, 85, 127, 141, 154
role-play 166, 169
room 15, 20, 32

safety 91
saturation 132
security 3, 25, 28, 29, 33, 34, 57, 102, 112
selection 41, 61, 71, 72, 106; of subjects 106; of themes 71, 72
selective reinforcement 111
selectivity 106, 120, 131
self-actualization 25, 27, 31–5
self-confidence 42, 48, 50, 138, 162, 165
self-control 41
self-criticism 79
self-deception 82
self-determination 15
self-disclosure 153
self-efficacy 67
self-esteem 50, 53
self-image 53
self-interest 21
self-motivation 49
self-protection 59, 83, 84
self-regulation 43, 48, 49
self-reliance 17
self-respect 149
sentiment 39, 40, 176
short-term help 77
silence(s) 92, 100, 101, 121
situation-clarification 92, 101, 118, 122, 124–7, 130, 133, 154
skills 1–4, 21, 33, 44, 45, 47, 48, 85, 87, 89–94, 102, 114, 116, 120, 122, 129, 133, 135, 145, 147, 151–4, 156–8, 165, 172, 178; arsenal of 129; assertiveness 45; basic 3, 90–2, 133; complex 3; differentiating 142; listening 92, 110; mental 90; micro 2; non-selective listening 92, 94, 106; regulating 92, 93, 122;

selective listening 92, 93, 106, 109
smile 98
social learning theory 23, 24, 41–3, 48, 80, 111, 135, 140
social skills 47, 171, 172, 177
solution 3, 4, 9, 12, 14, 15, 18, 19, 23, 24, 29, 32, 55, 56, 58, 59, 61, 72, 76, 77, 80, 81, 84, 91, 92, 94, 104, 106, 123, 125–8, 130, 138, 145
sophisticated 20
sophistication 30
sounding-board 58, 60
space 57, 70, 103–5, 107, 109, 121, 162
specification 119, 164
specificity 116
spontaneity 21, 27, 84
stage(s) 2, 3, 18, 30, 55, 68–77, 90, 94, 95, 106, 109, 116, 119, 123, 133–5, 140, 142, 144, 154, 158, 163, 165, 177, 178
standard(s) 26, 29, 39, 49, 51, 79, 81, 82, 85, 151, 161
starting the interview 92, 93, 95, 122
stigma 172
strategies for treatment 90, 135, 158
strategy/gies 57, 87
structure 94, 120, 122
suggestibility 108
suggestiveness 108
surface structure 117
suitability as a helper 78, 79
summarizing/summary 92, 102, 120–2, 126, 129, 131, 134, 142, 144, 147
summary of contents 120; of feelings 120
symptoms 150
system 4, 23; of norms 18; of theories 23

targets 51; realistic 51
teacher 65–7, 71, 140, 141, 172
termination 172, 175, 178
tests 142; paper-and-pencil 14; psychological 14

thinking 43, 49, 65; dysfunctional
  30; pattern 32; strategies 90;
  style of 42
thinking aloud 44, 64, 92, 122, 129,
  130
thought-associations 103
thoughts 18, 20, 26–31, 58, 63, 64,
  71, 100, 129, 130, 135, 138, 139,
  143, 151–3, 156, 157;
  interpreting 100
time 76, 78, 94, 122, 128, 131–3, 178
timing 122
tolerance of uncertainity 95, 104
tone 108, 109, 111, 112, 140, 143,
  146, 147; tentative 111, 112, 140
trait 42; hereditary 42
transfer of knowledge 45
treatment 3, 23, 158–60, 163, 165,
  167, 177; levels of 159, 163

treatment as education 167, 171
treatment of problem(s) 73, 77, 94,
  115, 119
trust 4, 10, 55, 57, 58, 70, 76, 115

unconditional positive regard 25–7,
  31
unmasking effect 145

vagueness(es) 118, 148
values 176
verbal fluency 31
verbal following 92, 99, 100, 104,
  105
vicious circle 50

warmth 25, 32

you-me-talk 154